POTPOURRI CRAFTS

POTPOURRI CRAFTS

MORE THAN 100 FRAGRANT RECIPES & PROJECTS FOR EVERY ROOM IN YOUR HOME

By Dawn Cusick

A Sterling/Lark Book

Sterling Publishing Co., Inc.   New York

To Gary — thanks for keeping such a great sense of humor about such a huge mess.

Special thanks to the following people who generously donated potpourri materials from their gardens: Nora and Fred Blose, Eula Haynes, Steffany LaBree, Cynthia Gillooly, Sylvia Tippett, Joyce Cusick, Bill and Dot Rosenstengel, James and Ruth Clark, Billie Rickman, Dot Bumpus, and Diane and Dick Weaver.

Photography: Evan Bracken, Light Reflections, Hendersonville, NC
Art Director: Marcia Winters
Production: Elaine Thompson, Elizabeth Albrecht, Sandra Montgomery
Illustrations: Diane Weaver
Editorial Assistance: Chris Rich, Steffany LaBree

Library of Congress Cataloging-in-Publication Data
Cusick, Dawn.
    Potpourri crafts : more than 100 fragrant recipes & projects for every room in your home / Dawn Cusick.
        p.   cm.
    Includes bibliographical references and index.
    ISBN 0-8069-8596-8
    1. Potpourris (Scented floral mixtures)   I. Title.
TT899.4.C87   1992
745.92--dc20   91-39269
                                                                                                      CIP

ISBN 0-8069-8596-8   Trade
        0-8069-8597-6   Paper

10 9 8 7 6 5 4 3

A Sterling/Lark Book

Produced by Altamont Press, Inc.
50 College Street, Asheville, NC 28801 USA

Published in 1992 by Sterling Publishing Co., Inc.
387 Park Avenue South, New York, NY 10016

Copyright 1992, Altamont Press

Distributed in Canada by Sterling Publishing
    c/o Canadian Manda Group, P.O. Box 920, Station U
    Toronto, Ontario, Canada M8Z 5P9
Distributed in the United Kingdom by Cassell PLC
    Villiers House, 41/47 Strand, London WC2N 5JE, England
Distributed in Australia by Capricorn Link Ltd., P.O. Box 665,
    Lane Cove, NSW 2066

Contents

Introduction

All crafters like the process of making something, and yet, for a variety of reasons, not all crafters like their finished products. Sometimes the techniques involved seem harder than anticipated; or the materials are so expensive that it's just too tempting to substitute materials of lesser quality; or maybe the directions promise results in two minutes and you simply run out of patience after two weeks and place the half-finished project in the trash; or, perhaps worst of all, the finished craft is lovely but what on earth do you do with it?

Whatever the reasons for a crafter's disappointment, it's important to remember that the strength of a crafter's creativity diminishes every time they begin a project with excitement and end up disliking the end result. The television set becomes more tempting than the work table; taking risks and learning new techniques no longer seems exciting; and faith is lost in the ability to add the personal touches that make each person's work truly special.

Like so many crafters, I've experienced that feeling of disappointment more times than I'd like to admit, but somewhere along the line I discovered that working with materials I find beautiful almost always yields beautiful results. If you've also been disappointed with some of your work, you will truly enjoy *Potpourri Crafts*. Beginning on page 18, you'll find more than 30 potpourri recipes, all photographed up close and reproduced in full color. It won't be difficult to find one whose beauty enchants you. (Or you can just bring home a lovely potpourri from the grocery store!)

Next, browse through the more than 100 projects that begin on page 54. The projects have been divided into chapters based on the average length of time each project takes to complete. In "Ten-Minute Miracles" you will find more than 40 projects that literally take ten minutes or less. "Afternoon Delights" introduces you to a range of projects that can be completed in several hours, and "All Day Affairs" features lovely projects that may take more than a few hours but are well worth the effort.

All of the projects include a complete materials list and step-by-step instructions. If the potpourri is not visible in the project, then the materials list suggests you use the potpourri of your choice. If the potpourri is visible, you are provided with a complete list of all the ingredients in that potpourri so you may replicate it if you wish. All of the projects in this book may be made with either store-bought or homemade potpourris. If you enjoy gardening, you will thrill to discover that making your own potpourri is a natural way to preserve your favorite flowers and herbs. Making homemade potpourri is also a viable option for non-gardeners. Instructions for making potpourri at home begin on pages 12 and 13.

Assembling the projects in this book was a real challenge. With the exception of potpourri sachets, which date back hundreds of years, potpourri crafts have not been around for long, and there really weren't any "specialists" or "experts" to turn to for help, only a few lone crafters who just love the fragrance and looks of potpourri and want to make something with it. As you look through the projects, you'll notice that not only is potpourri a craft in itself, but it also makes a wonderful complement to other crafts. Dollmaker Nora Blose, for example, enjoyed making potpourri purses and hats to accessorize her dolls, and professional framer Steffany LaBree had great fun working with shadow box frames and potpourri pictures.

My thanks go out to all of the designers who contributed to this book. After overcoming their initial skepticism with the potential of potpourri crafts, they plunged in with great zeal, and the success of their work is evident. You might be surprised, though, to learn that some of their most exciting ideas failed miserably. Had they stopped there, and not tried just one more time, they would have never experienced that incredible sense of satisfaction and energy that comes from making something ourselves and sharing that work with others. I wish you many such joyful moments as your begin making and enjoying your own potpourri crafts.

Dawn Cusick

Potpourris Through History

For today's connoisseur of potpourri who enjoys decorating with an antique bowl filled with a colorful, fragrant potpourri, the origins of potpourri may come as quite a surprise. While ancient potpourri recipes, like those of today, were usually revered for their fragrances, the fragrances were chosen because they were an easy way to cover up the unpleasant odors caused by rotting foods and poor sanitation or to ward off illness and insects.

The word potpourri comes from the French, and translates literally to "rotten pot." This translation refers to the ancient potpourris that were made by layering partially dried rose petals with salt to produce a caked base that was then cured with fixatives and spices. (While this method, known as the "moist method," makes a wonderfully fragrant potpourri, the fragrance dissipates quickly unless the potpourri is kept covered and it's not attractive enough to display.)

References to potpourri recipes and functions can be found in the writings of almost every culture and almost every time period: Desert dwellers in biblical times reputedly kept small bags of potpourri folded into their garments to keep insects from biting them while they slept; the Greeks placed small muslin bags of potpourri behind every guest at banquets; the early Egyptians buried their dead with potpourri; and the monks in medieval monasteries kept potpourri bags near the infirmary to speed the recoveries of their patients.

In the societies that followed, fragrance became a signifier of class and wealth. Each member of royalty had his or her own favorite potpourri: Louis XIV preferred a combination of nutmeg, jasmine, orange flowers, and cloves, while Queen Isabella of Spain preferred rose leaves, calamus, orris flowers, and coriander. Once a family had created a personal potpourri recipe, everything from bed sheets to clothing to candles to jewelry, soap, and writing inks would be saturated with that fragrance. A family's fragrance was almost as important as its crest, and homes in 16th-century England were often built with a "stillroom" where fragrant flowers and herbs from the garden were hung up to dry and then mixed into potpourris and bouquets.

While the art of creating family fragrances in a stillroom may have disappeared, one could easily argue that fragrance is every bit as valued today as it was in the 16th century. Perfumes and colognes are purchased every year by the thousands; store shelves are lined with aerosol sprays and other creative concoctions to add fragrance and disguise everyday odors in the home; and potpourri is now manufactured in mass in designer fragrances and colors. The more things change, the more they stay the same.

Popular Potpourri Ingredients

FRAGRANT MATERIALS

Fragrant plants and spices have always been and still are the most popular ingredients in potpourri. These materials can include any number of fragrant flowers, herbs, and spices, including roses, lavender, scented geranium, basil, star anise, and cinnamon, just to name a few.

DECORATIVE MATERIALS

As fragrant oils have become more accessible and reasonably priced, decorative, non-fragrant materials have become popular potpourri ingredients. Colorful whole blossoms and leaves make especially interesting additions to potpourris that are displayed in bowls or crafts.

WOOD SHAVINGS

Large shavings of wood are abundant in commercially-made potpourris because they make inexpensive filler material and absorb the fragrance from essential oils well. For homemade potpourris, the delicate curls of wood shavings from craftsmen are lovely additions. They blend naturally with flowers and leaves and also absorb essential oils well.

FIXATIVES

Since most natural fragrances have a relatively short life span, fixatives are often added to homemade potpourris. Fixatives are natural materials that absorb and hold the fragrances they are exposed to. Many fixatives have a fragrance of their own, so you will want to be sure it is compatible with other fragrances in your potpourri. Several types of fixatives can be mixed in a potpourri as long as you find their combined fragrances pleasing. For a homemade potpourri, you will need approximately one tablespoon of powdered fixative for each cup of potpourri. Orrisroot, gum benzoin resin, tonka beans, vetiver root, sandalwood bark, and patchouli leaves are several of the most popular fixatives. Since you will probably have to rely on mail order sources to find them, you may want to order small quantities of each type so you can discover which ones and combinations you like best.

OILS

Fragrant oils (also called essential oils) are so versatile that you will probably be tempted to begin a collection. If you're making potpourri in the traditional way, fragrant oils are added to the potpourri before it's left to cure. Fragrant oils are also a quick way to add fragrance to a potpourri made from colorful but unscented materials, or to refresh the fragrance of an older potpourri.

Where To Find Potpourri Ingredients

GROW THEM

Growing your own materials is perhaps the easiest and least expensive way to find ingredients for your potpourris, and you'll find your garden a constant source of inspiration for new potpourri recipes. Surprisingly, though, some gardeners find it too painful to harvest the flowers and herbs they've nourished through the season. For these gardeners there's always the possibility of planting an extra bed of plants just for potpourri or collecting petals and leaves from the ground after a rain or windstorm.

SCAVENGE FOR THEM

A true potpourri lover has no pride, and will scavenge for potpourri ingredients anytime and anywhere the opportunity presents itself. When you're visiting friends and walking through their gardens, look on the ground at the base of their plants for fallen petals and seed pods. The next time you're in a florist's shop, peak into the bottom of their cooler for interesting flowers and leaves — you may be surprised at how helpful flower-lovers are when they know their discarded materials will be appreciated and given new life. Plant nurseries are another place for great finds — just wander down the aisles with your eyes focused on the ground for fallen spoils. (They'll think you're weird but you'll have the last laugh.) Hiking and picnic excursions are an obvious time to look for potpourri materials, although many people forget to look in the fall and winter when seed pods and other interesting materials are in abundance.

PURCHASE THEM

A wide variety of single potpourri ingredients can be ordered in small, inexpensive quantities from mail order sources. (See page 143.) Even if your garden is bountiful and you're a great success at scavenging, it's still fun to order materials indigenous to other parts of the country and materials with fascinating names (deer's tongue, for example) that you've never seen before.

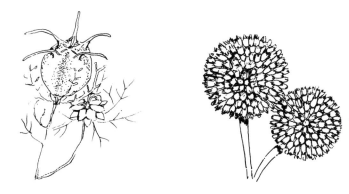

Making Potpourri From Scratch

PREPARING THE MATERIALS

All of the materials in your potpourri will need to be completely dry. Once a plant's natural moisture is gone, the flowers and leaves will feel crispy, almost like breakfast cereal. Many flowers and leaves will shrink as they dry, and you shouldn't be too disappointed if the brilliant colors in your fresh flowers fade as they dry. Always pick flowers and leaves for drying on a sunny day, after the moisture from dew or rain has dried.

Most materials that are dried for fragrance can simply be spread out on paper towels and turned every few days until they are dry. This method has several drawbacks, though. If you live in a very humid environment, the materials may not ever dry completely, and blossoms with any weight to them may dry lopsided. Alternative methods of drying are discussed below, and since none of them require great technical knowledge or expense, you should always feel free to experiment with them to achieve the best results.

SCREEN DRYING

This method is ideal if you live in a humid area or want a bloom to dry without losing its shape. Simply prepare a piece of metal screen by elevating it on bricks, books, or anything else you have handy. Single leaves and petals should be placed flat on the screen, while whole blooms and seed heads should be positioned with their stems falling through a hole in the screen with their best side facing upwards. Allow at least a half inch (1-1/4 cm.) of space around each item to ensure good ventilation. Leaves should be turned every few days.

HANG DRYING

Hang drying is a quick way to dry large amounts of sturdy materials. With this method, four to six stems of an herb or flower are tied loosely together and then hung upside down in a dark, dry area for two to four weeks. When the drying process is complete, simply separate blooms and leaves from the stems. Statice (annual, German, and caspia), love-in-a-mist, lavender, and silver king artemisia all dry well with this method.

SILICA GEL DRYING

Drying with silica gel (and other desiccants such as sand, borax, and kitty litter) can provide you with stunning, colorful blooms to top off a potpourri. Many of the flowers that will dry in desiccants just will not dry with other methods without turning brown. Don't be turned off by the initial expense — used silica gel crystals can be baked in the oven and then reused.

Dry with silica gel by sprinkling about an inch (2-1/2 cm.) of the crystals onto the bottom of a cardboard box. Position the blooms on top of the silica gel so that no petals overlap, and then sprinkle another inch of silica gel over the blooms. Continue layering silica gel and flowers until the box is full or you exhaust your materials. Drying times vary, but the average range is three to seven days. Pansies, violets, zinnias, and daisies dry especially well with silica gel.

Note: As innocent as it looks, silica gel is toxic, and care should be taken not to inhale any of the fine dust which may arise as you layer it over flowers. Wash your hands after each exposure, and avoid the temptation to work in the kitchen. (It could easily be mistaken for sugar!) Always store your boxes of drying blooms on a high shelf, well out of reach of curious children.

HOW TO MAKE A POTPOURRI

Once your materials are dry you are ready to begin assembling a base of fragrant materials in a bowl. You can choose materials with the same type of fragrance or mix and match to create a completely individual fragrance. Some commonly recognized categories of fragrance include floral fragrances (roses, scented geraniums, honeysuckle), fresh fragrances (lavender, rosemary), spicy fragrances (allspice, cinnamon, star anise, nutmeg, cloves), and citrus fragrances (lemon verbena, lemon balm, lemon basil, lemon, lime, and orange peel).

When you're happy with the fragrance of your base, it's time to make your potpourri look pretty. (See "Potpourris Featuring Color" and "Potpourris Featuring Shape and Texture" on pages 32 and 46.) The materials you choose should complement the surroundings where the potpourri will be displayed. This may sound complicated, but actually it's quite fun. If the potpourri is for the dining room table and your favorite tablecloth is embroidered with delicate pansies, then you may want to arrange several pansies on the top of your potpourri. If the potpourri is for a bathroom and you've just redecorated in mauve, you'll enjoy finding flowers like statice and globe amaranth that are just the right color.

Now it's time to "fix" the fragrance. For each cup of potpourri you've made, sprinkle about a tablespoon of fixative over the dry materials. You now have the option of adding a few drops of fragrant oil to the potpourri if you'd like a stronger or different fragrance. Be sure to use only a few drops — you can add more later if the scent is too weak. Mix the potpourri well with your fingers or a plastic or wooden spoon and place the potpourri in a brown paper bag. Roll it up tightly so there's no extra air and shake well. Place in a dark location and shake once a day for a week; then shake once a week for five weeks. Remove the potpourri from the bag and enjoy!

Materials, Tips, and Traps

MATERIALS

You are probably already familiar with the materials used in potpourri crafts. They include glue, fabric, lace, tulle, ribbon, corsage pins, and foam. Fortunately, these materials are pretty to look at, fun to work with, and usually not obscure or expensive.

■ Craft glues, tacky glues, adhesive sprays, and hot or low melt glues all work well. Although a specific type of glue is usually called for in each project's instructions, you should feel free to use whatever you have on hand and works best for you. If you choose to use a glue gun, be sure to keep safety in mind: it is deceptively easy for the glue to saturate fabric, lace, or tulle and cause bad burns.

■ Foam is often used as a base in potpourri crafts. The foam is simply covered with craft glue or spray adhesive and covered with potpourri.

■ Fine wedding netting, tulle, and lace are available in a variety of colors and make lovely, fragrant sachets.

■ Corsage Pins are used to attach small sachets to foam bases and allow for easy removal.

TIPS

■ Keep proportions in mind when choosing display bowls and baskets: potpourris with very large ingredients look out of place in small bowls, and potpourris with very small, delicate materials look lost in large, rustic baskets.

■ If you'd like to display your favorite potpourri in a large bowl or basket but don't have enough to fill it, simply line the bottom of the container with newspaper or tissue paper and then cover completely with potpourri.

■ Narrow satin ribbons make lovely accents in potpourri crafts and can be embellished with tiny love knots or small blooms from a potpourri.

■ When your potpourri's fragrance begins to fade, try placing it in a moist room, such as a bathroom or kitchen. Moisture releases the natural fragrance of many plants.

TRAPS

■ Potpourris displayed on a window sill or other sunny location will quickly lose their color.

■ Never display potpourri near an open widow or in the path of a fan.

■ Make sure all of your potpourri ingredients are really dry before mixing them together or uninvited mold will appear.

■ The fragrant oils used in commercially made potpourris (and some homemade potpourris) often leave stains on wood, fabric, and even walls. Cotton liners can be sewn in your sachets if the fabric is thin or of great value to you, and felt liners can be applied to the bottom of display bowls or the backs of wreaths.

■ Be sure to keep display potpourris and potpourri crafts out of reach of curious toddlers.

Making Sachets

The popularity of the sachet dates back to early Greece, when small muslin sachets were placed by each guest at banquets. (This tradition continued through the centuries into the late 1700s.) Also known as 'sweet bags', sachets can be filled with any combination of fragrant dried materials that you find pleasing. Henry the III's sachets were filled with violets, roses, sandalwood, cloves, coriander, and lavender, while Queen Isabella of Spain preferred coriander, orris flowers, calamus, and roses.

Historically, sachets were filled with materials that had been crushed with a mortar and pestle into a fine powder. Today's sachets are usually filled with regular potpourri, thus allowing you to rejuvenate the sachet's fragrance every few months by simply squeezing the sachet.

The basic sachet is very simple to make, requiring only two side seams. (The seams can also be secured with hot glue if you'd rather not sew.) Almost any fabric will work, although sachets made from natural fiber fabrics (such as cotton, silk, or linen) tend to release fragrance better.

STEP-BY-STEP . . .

1. Photo copy the sachet patterns on pages 140 and 141 and cut them out. Fold the fabric in half, right sides together. Position the pattern on the fold as the arrows indicate. Pin the pattern to the fabric and cut out.

2. Remove the pattern and pin the side seams together. Sew with a 1/4-inch seam allowance. Turn the sachet right sides out and press well. Press the top of the sachet under 1/4-inch and sew. Then press the top of the sachet under another inch (2.5 cm.).

3. Fill the bag three-fourths full with potpourri and tie it closed with ribbon. Tip: If you're working with a very thin or cherished piece of fabric and your potpourri contains essential oils, you may want to make a small pouch out of netting and then place the pouch inside the sachet to prevent fabric stains.

4. The finished sachet is now ready to be decorated with satin ribbon, dried flowers, dried herbs, whole spices, gathered lace, silk flowers, or any combination of the above. All of these materials can be attached to the sachet in seconds with a glue gun.

Making Sleep Pillows

The lines of distinction between sachets and sleep pillows are often nebulous. Sleep pillows tend to be slightly larger in size, they are usually sewn shut on all sides, and they can be edged with ruffles, lace, or piping. The heart sachet shown here, for example, is assembled like a pillow but would universally be accepted as a sachet. Regardless of how they are defined, sleep pillows are a wonderful way to add delicate fragrance around your home, and you can move them around from room to room as needed. Their small size invites additions of lace and ruffles, and the top surface area is an ideal place to showcase antique laces and special needlework skills.

The first sleep pillows were made by the Romans, who filled them with dried rose petals. Through the centuries that followed, pillows were also filled with hops (to induce sleep), lavender (to fragrance a sick room), rosemary (to free the sleeper from evil dreams), and cloves (to prevent snoring).

STEP-BY-STEP . . .

1. Photocopy the pillow patterns on pages 140 and 141 and cut them out. (Note: You can also make your own patterns by tracing the shape of a box or a plate.)

2. Method A — Use this method when working with antique fabrics and laces.

■ Cut two to four layers of quilt batting from the pattern and pin it to the wrong side of the pillow's bottom piece. Experiment with the number of batting layers until you're happy with the thickness.

■ Pin the two pillow pieces together, right sides together, and sew the seams. Leave a 2- to 3-inch (5- to 7-cm.) opening.

■ Cut two layers of tulle or netting slightly smaller than the pattern. Top-stitch the netting together on three sides, fill with potpourri, and then top-stitch the last side.

■ Slide this potpourri pouch into the pillow and sew the opening closed by hand. This seam can be re-opened later to launder the pillow or to add a fresh pouch of potpourri.

2. Method B — Use this method when speed is your main concern.

■ Pin the two pillow pieces together, right sides together, and sew the seams. Leave a 2- to 3-inch opening.

■ Fill the potpourri with small pieces of fiberfill and potpourri until you're happy with the fullness. Sew the opening closed by hand.

3. To add a ruffle, cut a length of lace or fabric twice as long as the pillow's sides. Gather the lace or fabric with a running stitch (or use pre-gathered lace). Hem the ruffle if needed. Position the lace between the two pieces of fabric with the gathered edge flush with the outer edges of the fabric. (See illustration.) Sew seams as usual.

Potpourris Featuring Natural Fragrance

The availability of inexpensive essential oils has made creating a potpourri with fragrance as simple as adding a few drops of liquid to a bowl of dried petals. Creating a potpourri with a natural, more personal fragrance, however, is a bit more challenging.

So how do you know which ingredients to choose for a naturally fragrant potpourri? It helps if you have a theme in mind before you begin creating the recipe: the potpourri's fragrance, for example, could be floral, spicy, woodsy, or clean. First choose your base ingredient, something with a scent you really enjoy, and then add materials with complemetary fragrances. Keep in mind that when several fragrant materials are combined together it often creates an entirely new fragrance, and that the fixative you choose may also affect the final fragrance. Some potpourris will need the addition of colorful, textured materials to increase visual appeal.

As time passes, you can rejuvenate the natural fragrance of your potpourri by crumbling a few of the flowers and leaves between your fingers or by adding fresh fragrant materials, and there's nothing dishonorable about adding a few drops of a compatible essential oil to refresh the potpourri.

LAVENDER

MINIATURE
ROSEBUDS

ORRIS ROOT

19

DRIED APPLE SLICES

ROSE HIPS

STAR ANISE

CLOVES

JUNIPER BERRIES

SWEET GUM BALLS
& BARK

PINE NEEDLES

RED PEPPERS

CINNAMON STICKS

OAK MOSS

ASSORTED SEED BALLS
& PODS

ESSENTIAL OILS

MARJORAM

ALLSPICE BERRIES

CLOVES

SPICE BASIL

STAR ANISE

HONEY LOCUST LEAVES

BUTTERCUPS

VETIVER

PINE WOOD SHAVINGS

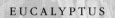

EUCALYPTUS

SANDALWOOD

HIBISCUS

ANNUAL STATICE

22

TREE TRIMMINGS

BAY LEAVES

LAVENDER BUDS

CLOVES

ORRISROOT

ORANGE RIND

CANELLA BERRIES

LEMON BASIL

LEMON VERBENA

ORANGE TREE BLOOMS

ORANGE PEEL

CINNAMON BASIL

CINNAMON CHIPS

ALLSPICE BERRIES

JASMINE BLOSSOMS

PANSIES
(you occupy my thoughts)

WHITE DAISIES
(innocence)

HIBISCUS
(delicate beauty)

MINT
(virtue)

FERN
(sincerity)

RED SALVIA
(forever thine)

Potpourris Featuring Symbolic Meaning

Centuries ago, before the days when row after row of greeting cards were avilable to express the perfect sentiment on a special occasion, flowers and herbs were combined together to create gift bouquets and potpourris for sleep pillows. The Victorians were so well versed in the historical meanings of these flowers and herbs that they used them to create the most intricate messages to loved ones and enemies.

If a Victorian woman saw her lover flirting with someone else, she might send him a tussie mussie of foxgloves (to symbolize insincerity), marigolds (to symbolize despair), and rosemary (to symbolize remembrance). Many Victorians also believed that the contents of one's dreams could be influenced by the symbolic meanings of the flowers and herbs in the potpourri they choose to fill their sleep pillows. So if you wanted to dream about a cherished spouse who was out of town, you might fill a sleep pillow with red salvia (to symbolize that they were forever thine), ivy (to symbolize friendship and fidelity), and sweet basil (to symbolize good wishes).

The recipes on the following pages can be copied to create gifts for special people in your life, or you can mix and match the flowers and herbs to create your own meaningful potpourris.

A Potpourri to Reprimand a Cheating Lover

PINK LARKSPUR
(fickleness)

LAVENDER
(distrust)

LOVE-IN-A-MIST
(perplexity)

MARIGOLDS
(grief, despair)

MAPLE
(reserve)

PURPLE LARKSPUR
(haughtiness)

FOXGLOVE
(insincerity)

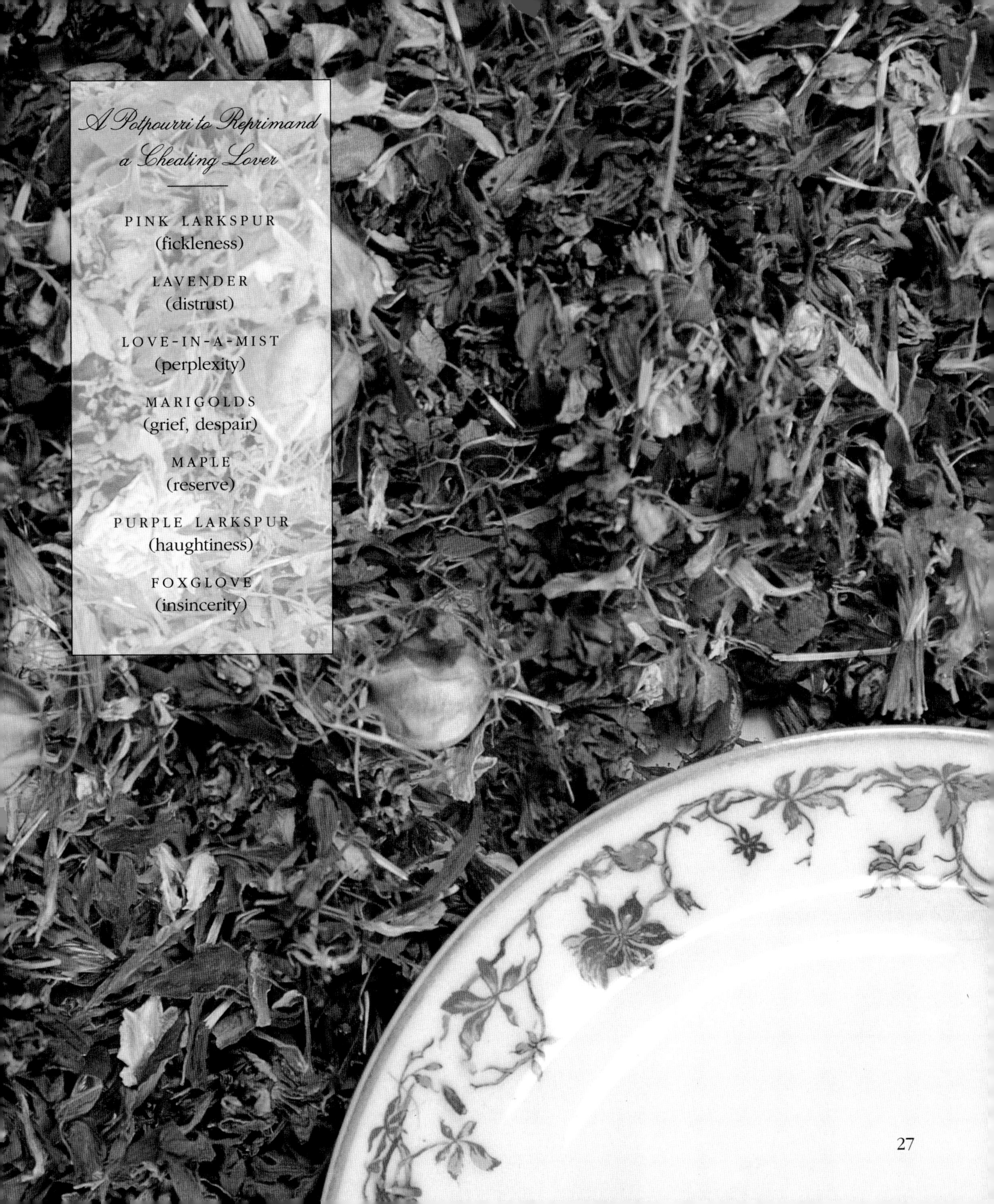

A Potpourri to
Celebrate a New Home

CEDAR
(strength)

CHAMOMILE
(energy in adversity)

LOCUST
(elegance)

SAGE
(domestic virtue)

EUCALYPTUS
(protection)

28

A Potpourri to Encourage Sweet Dreams

PEPPERMINT AND
SPEARMINT
(warmth of feeling)

ROSEMARY
(remembrance)

LEMON BALM
(zest)

HONESTY
(sincerity)

CHRISTMAS ROSES
(relieve my anxiety)

29

A Potpourri to
Celebrate a Birth

———

HONEYSUCKLE
(sweetness of disposition,
bonds of love)

MOSS
(maternal love)

PARSLEY
(festivity)

PUSSY WILLOWS
(unrealized promise)

BACHELOR'S-BUTTON
(single blessedness)

A Potpourri to Celebrate a Graduation

SWEET BASIL
(good wishes)

SCOTCH FIR
(elevation)

SAFFRON
(beware of success)

HOLLY
(foresight)

CHERRY BLOOMS
(good education)

31

Potpourris Featuring Color

Once upon a time, more than a thousand years ago, potpourris were created only with fragrance in mind. And since most naturally fragrant materials lack in vibrant color, most of these historical potpourris were not all that exciting to look at. Today, color plays an important role in what people look for in a potpourri. Stores are filled with potpourris in the latest designer colors, from peach to mauve to bright purple. These colors are relatively easy to achieve with synthetic dyes, and the potpourris still have a strong fragrance thanks to a good soaking in essential oils.

If you've decided to make your own potpourri at home with materials from your garden, you may be surprised at the incredible rainbow of colors available naturally. The group of flowers called "everlastings" are easy to grow and provide a wide range of colors. Annual statice, strawflowers, and globe amaranth are included in this group, but many other herbs, leaves, and flowers also maintain their brilliant colors after they dry.

Try to combine materials with subtle variations in shading to prevent the individual blooms from merging into one big blob of color. Fragrance can be added with a few drops of essential oil or by adding fragrant flowers and a fixative to your potpourri. To prevent the colors from fading, be sure not to display the potpourri in a location where it will receive direct

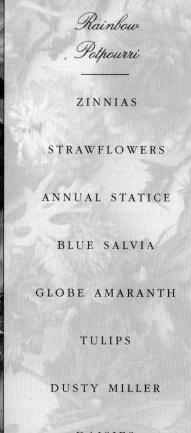

Rainbow Potpourri

ZINNIAS

STRAWFLOWERS

ANNUAL STATICE

BLUE SALVIA

GLOBE AMARANTH

TULIPS

DUSTY MILLER

DAISIES

Pink
Potpourri

———

LARKSPUR

ZINNIAS

STRAWFLOWERS

CELOSIA

GLOBE AMARANTH

RAT TAIL STATICE

COCKSCOMB

ACHILLEA
'THE PEARL'

TULIPS

33

*Silver
Potpourri*

———

LAMB'S EAR

PUSSY WILLOWS

SAGE

SILVER KING
ARTEMISIA

DUSTY MILLER

GLOBE THISTLE

Purple
Potpourri
———

LAVENDER

PINCUSHION FLOWER

LARKSPUR

BLUE SALVIA

BACHELOR'S-BUTTONS

GLOBE THISTLE

Cream
Potpourri

STRAWFLOWERS

GLOBE AMARANTH

PEARLY
EVERLASTING

HYDRANGEA

COCKSCOMB

ROSEBUDS

YARROW

BELLS-OF-IRELAND

Gold

Potpourri

CALENDULA

ZINNIAS

MARIGOLDS

PANSIES

CELOSIA

BLACK-EYED SUSANS

TIGER LILIES

DAFFODILS

TANSY

37

Magenta
Potpourri

———

STRAWFLOWERS

ROSES

GLOBE AMARANTH

TULIPS

ZINNIAS

Green
Potpourri

———

BAY LEAVES

SWEET MARJORAM

OAK LEAF HYDRANGEA
FOLIAGE

URA URSI LEAVES

DEER'S TONGUE

SPEARMINT LEAVES

CINNAMON BASIL

SPICE BASIL

OREGANO

PARSLEY

CHIVES

SWEET MARJORAM

ORNAMENTAL PEPPERS

Potpourris Featuring Function

By virtue of their fragrance and beauty, all potpourris are functional, yet some potpourris are created for other reasons. The ingredients in culinary potpourris, for example, serve as inspiration to creative cooks and can be removed from their display containers to flavor a meal at any time. (Just be sure that all of the ingredients were carefully washed before drying and that none were dried in toxic desiccants.)

Potpourris can also be made from the wonderful variety of herbs revered through history for their ability to repel insects or revitalize the skin and spirits. The recipes on the following pages offer you an inviting array of potpourris to appreciate for their practical uses as well as their fragrance and looks.

*Culinary
Potpourri*

———

CILANTRO

BLACK AND WHITE
PEPPERCORNS

BLACK PEPPER

SAFFRON

MUSTARD SEEDS

DEHYDRATED PEAS

Bath Potpourri

BEE BALM

ROSE PETALS

LAVENDER

PEPPERMINT

COMFREY

LEMON VERBENA

CHAMOMILE

BEE BALM BLOOMS

SCENTED
GERANIUM LEAVES

PEPPERMINT

Flea Repellant
Potpourri

———

SOUTHERNWOOD

SILVER KING
ARTEMISIA

PENNYROYAL
BLOOMS AND FOLIAGE

44

PURPLE
CONEFLOWERS

ACHILLEA
'THE PEARL'

TANSY

SILVER KING
ARTEMISIA

SOUTHERNWOOD

PENNYROYAL

45

Potpourris Featuring Shape and Texture

Potpourri materials with interesting shapes and textures add a wonderful, exhilarating allure to display potpourris. This tactile dimension of something so traditionally associated with fragrance seems to send imaginations reeling. People gaze into the potpourri and wonder. . . Are the tips of those globe thistles really as prickly as they look? How would one of these lamb's ear leaves feel on my cheek? Would anyone get mad if I stuck my hands into the bowl and played with the wild basil seed heads?

Although most materials with interesting shapes and textures have little or no natural fragrance, a few drops of essential oil can easily add a favorite scent to the potpourri. Velvety spires of blue salvia, lacy Queen Anne's lace, and feathery soft celosia are just a few of many options. When creating your own recipes, remember that these   materials often showcase best against a neutral background—such as ordinary leaves— and that the larger size of many of these materials means they are best displayed in larger containers.

QUEEN ANNE'S LACE

RAT TAIL STATICE

CONE ALDER

MOSS

ACORNS

MAPLE LEAVES

POPPY HEADS

FIRE THORN
BERRIES

ASSORTED PODS
AND SEED HEADS

48

JASMINE

GLOBE AMARANTH
FOLIAGE

MOUNTAN MINT
SEED HEADS

BLACK-EYED SUSAN
SEED HEADS

49

PUSSY WILLOWS

CHENILLE BLOOMS

BLUE SALVIA

LEMON VERBENA

STRAWFLOWERS

ROSES

BACHELOR'S-BUTTONS

LARKSPUR

LEMON GRASS

PEPPERBERRIES

ORRIS ROOT

SUNFLOWER PETALS,
HEAD, AND SEEDS

LEMON VERBENA
LEAVES AND OIL

HONESTY

STRAWFLOWERS

CARNATIONS

CANELLA BERRIES

JUNIPER

LAMB'S EAR

GOLDENROD

ALLIUM

Ten-Minute Miracles

Decorated with potpourri, these small bath soaps create a lovely accessory for the bathroom and take less than five minutes to make.

MATERIALS: Potpourri of your choice (lavender was used in the soaps shown here), small bath soaps (available in department stores), craft glue

STEPS: **1** Apply a thick layer of craft glue to the soap on the places you want the potpourri to be. Sprinkle the potpourri over the glue and gently press in place with your index finger. Allow to dry completely and then shake off any potpourri that didn't stick to the glue.
2 Select several special blooms from the potpourri (miniature rosebuds and celosia blooms were used here) and glue them in or around the potpourri on the soaps. Allow to dry completely before arranging the soaps in a dish or bowl of potpourri.

Tip: Since you're working with small soaps, the materials in the potpourri should be proportionately small.

Available in a variety of shapes, foam wreath bases can be covered with a decorative layer of fragrant potpourri in just a few minutes.

MATERIALS: Purchased potpourri (apple and peach scents were used in the wreaths shown here), heart-shaped foam wreath bases, craft glue

STEPS: **1** Apply a generous layer of craft glue to the base. Gently press the potpourri into the glue and allow to dry completely.
2 Examine the wreath for bare spots and cover with a second layer of potpourri if necessary.

Grow Your Own Lavender

Of the 20 species of lavender, English lavender (Lavandula vera) offers the most aromatic oil, but many other species of this half-hardy perennial are also fragrant. The Romans and Greeks used lavender to perfume their baths, and it was also prized for its reputed medicinal qualities.

Taller species are ideal in hedges, while shorter ones serve well in borders. Lavender's narrow leaves are grayish-green in color, and its small flowers are clustered in spikes. Colors range from violet to blue to lilac, pink, and white. Easy to propagate from cuttings, lavender prefers light, moderately dry soil and full sun.

Dry by hanging in small bunches.

Old toys make great containers for displaying a children's potpourri. And what, you may ask, is in a children's potpourri? Crayon and colored pencil shavings if you're lucky; snake skins and bug carcasses if you're not!

MATERIALS: Crayon shavings, colored pencil shavings, wood shavings, essential oil of your choice

STEPS: **1** Fill a plastic container about half full with wood shavings. Add several drops of essential oil, place the top on the container, and allow to sit for three days. **2** Add crayon and colored pencil shavings, stir well, and display in a creative container.

Easter baskets are for adults, too, and this one makes a fragrant gift for yourself or your favorite bunny.

MATERIALS: Potpourri of your choice, foam egg shapes, craft glue, Easter basket, iridescent grass, large bow, assorted candy

STEPS: **1** Apply a generous layer of craft glue to each foam egg and gently press the potpourri into the glue. Allow to dry completely. Examine the eggs for bare spots and cover with another layer of potpourri if necessary. **2** Fill the basket with grass, potpourri eggs, and candy, and tie a large bow to the handle.

Grow Your Own Rosemary

Rosemary enjoys a long list of reputed powers: over time it has been thought to stimulate hair growth (combs were made of its wood), aid the memory (students in ancient Greece wore it while they studied for exams), reform thieves (after soaking their feet in rosemary vinegar), soothe aching joints, prevent bad dreams, and protect its wearers from the plague.

Today it is used primarily as a culinary herb, and in shampoos and potpourris.

A half-hardy evergreen, Rosemary (Rosmarinus officinalis) is an ornamental bush. The plants grown best in light, well-drained soil, and are easy to propagate from cuttings.

Dry by spacing stems on a screen drying rack.

If you have an interesting collection of herbs and spices in your kitchen cupboard but find yourself forgetting to use them, try mixing your favorites into a potpourri and displaying them on a counter top in a pretty glass jar. The potpourri shown here was made from equal amounts of sweet marjoram, rosemary, parsley, oregano, fennel, and tarragon.

Grow Your Own Sage

Originally a Mediterranean plant, the French used sage as a moth repellant and the Chinese often traded three pounds of their own tea leaves for a pound of sage leaves from Holland.

Common sage (Salvia officinalis) has attractive, wooly foliage that is gray-green in color. The plants produce short spikes of purple, blue, or white flowers. Sage can be prop-agated from seed, cuttings, or division. It prefers well-drained soil, a winter mulch, and plenty of sun.

Dry by hanging in small bunches or by spreading individual leaves flat on a screen rack.

These charming herb dolls are made with bouquets of dried herbs and accessorized with potpourri hats and baskets.

MATERIALS: Potpourri of your choice, rubber band, miniature basket and straw hat, narrow satin ribbon, approximately 30 stems of dried wormwood, sweet Annie, southernwood, annual statice, peppergrass, wild grasses, and strawflowers in any combination, corsage pins, craft glue

STEPS: **1** Arrange the herbs into a fan shape. Layer additional stems of blooms until you are satisfied with the bouquet's fullness. Secure the bouquet together at the top of the stems with a rubber band. **2** Arrange the miniature hat so it covers the rubber band and secure it in place with a corsage pin. Tie colorful strands of narrow satin ribbon around the hat and then around the basket's handle. **3** Fill the miniature basket with fragrant potpourri. Last, use craft glue to decorate the rim of the hat with potpourri.

Grow Your Own Blue Salvia

Originally from the mountains of Mexico, blue salvia (Salvia azurea) makes a lovely garden plant. Its graceful leaves are narrow and gray-green in color, and the flowers bloom from mid to late summer.

A hardy perennial, blue salvia can tolerate both drought and poor soil, but does require plenty of sun. Propagate the plants from cuttings or seeds, and cut them back each year.

Dry the flowers by hanging in small bunches or on a screen rack.

Scented geranium leaves, beebalm blooms, and several varieties of mint make a lovely potpourri to display, or a delicious homemade tea.

Potpourri booties are a darling way to decorate baby shower gifts or fragrance baby's clothing and take only minutes to make.

MATERIALS: Potpourri of your choice, pair of baby booties, craft glue, glue gun

STEPS: **1** Stuff the toes and ankles of each bootie with potpourri.
2 When the bootie is completely full, adhere the top pieces of potpourri to the sides of the bootie with craft glue. Last, choose several whole blooms and glue them on top of the potpourri.
3 Hot-glue narrow ribbon streamers or bows to the booties.

Decorating packages with small, lacy sachets adds excitement to every gift occasion.

MATERIALS FOR THE CIRCLE SACHET: Potpourri of your choice, small embroidery hoop, lace ribbon and fabric, narrow satin ribbon, craft glue

STEPS: **1** Cut two pieces of lace fabric slightly larger than each of the hoop's two circles. Glue one piece of lace to each circle, folding the edges down over the sides. **2** Glue a length of gathered lace (or gather it as you go) to the bottom side of the top hoop. Allow to dry completely. **3** Fill the bottom hoop with potpourri and gently position it inside the top hoop, adjusting the tension as necessary. Decorate with narrow ribbon and attach to the package with tape or a dab of glue.

MATERIALS FOR THE HEART SACHET: Potpourri of your choice, lace fabric and ribbon, satin ribbon, small silk flowers, craft glue

Follow the general instructions on pages 16 and 17 for making a heart sachet. Decorate the finished sachet with ribbon and silk flowers, and then attach it to the package with tape or a dab of glue.

68

Two distinct plants lay claim to the common name of chamomile: Anthemis nobilis (Roman chamomile) and Matricaria chamomilla (German chamomile). Though distinctively different in size and shape, both plants have feathery leaves, apple-like aromas, and surprisingly similar commercial uses in sedatives and tonics.

Roman chamomile is a low-growing hardy perennial requiring well-drained soil and full sun. It can be propagated by runners or root division. The plants spread rapidly and create wonderfully fragrant lawns in moist climates. The small cream-colored flower heads may be picked three or four times a year.

German chamomile is a tall annual best propagated from seed. The flowers are not as fragrant as Roman chamomile, but are widely used in the cosmetic industry.

Dry the flowers by hanging in small bunches or by arranging individual flower heads on a screen rack.

Kissing balls were a valued part of the flirtatious frolicking enjoyed by the leisure class in Victorian England, and while they may not inspire romance today, they do make pretty tree ornaments and fragrant accents around the home.

MATERIALS FOR LAVENDER KISSING BALL (left): Lavender, lavender oil, 2-inch (5-cm.) foam ball, two colors of narrow satin ribbon, craft glue

STEPS: **1** Cover the foam ball with glue using a paint brush or your finger. Roll the ball in lavender, allow to dry, and glue on additional lavender to cover bare spots if necessary. **2** Divide the ball into quarters with the ribbons and tie them together at the top of the ball to form a hanger. Add several drops of lavender oil.

MATERIALS FOR ROSEBUD KISSING BALL (right): Miniature rose buds, crushed thyme, rose oil, 2-inch (5-cm.) foam ball, five colors of narrow satin ribbon, sewing pins, craft glue

STEPS: **1** Cover the foam ball with glue using a paint brush or your finger. Roll the ball in thyme, allow to dry, and glue on additional thyme to cover bare spots if necessary. **2** Cut a 6-inch (15-cm.) length of satin ribbon and secure it to the top of the ball with sewing pins and hot glue to form the hanger. Cut additional lengths of narrow ribbon to form the streamers and secure to the bottom of the ball with sewing pins and hot glue. Embellish the streamers with rose buds and knots. **3** Begin hot-gluing rose buds around the hanger and work your way down and around the ball until you've covered about three-fourths of the ball. Scent with a few drops of rose oil.

Sachets filled with a moth-repellant potpourri are valued for their function, yet they can also be made as decorative as desired in any number of shapes and fabrics.

Materials for the moth-repellant potpourri can be found on page 45 and complete instructions for making the sachets can be found on page 16.

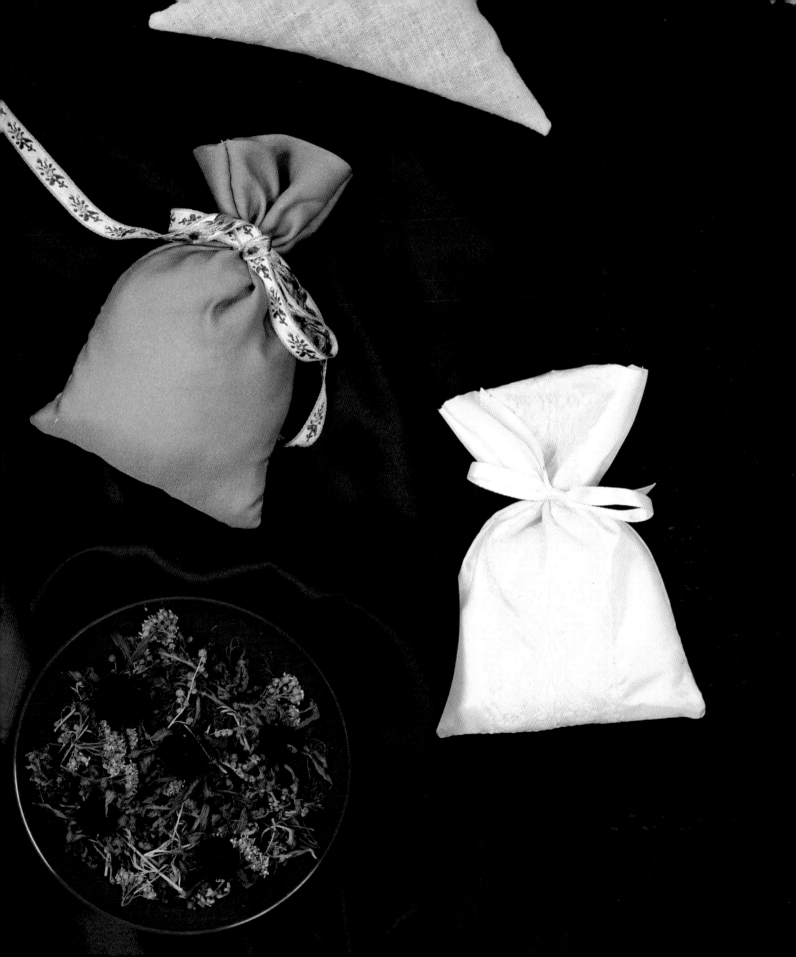

Sachets filled with a flea-repellant potpourri are simple to make and can be tucked into the bedding of a favorite pet.

MATERIALS: Flea-repellant potpourri (see page 44 for recipe), cotton or other natural-fiber fabric

Cut the fabric into two squares. Fill the center of one square with potpourri and top-stitch the second square on top of the first one.

Decorating your bathroom can be as simple as filling a basket with coordinating sachets.

MATERIALS: Potpourri of your choice, basket, wash cloths, narrow satin ribbon

Position the wash cloths right side down on a flat surface. Place about 1/2 cup (125 ml.) of potpourri in the center of each cloth. Gather the cloths up and around the potpourri and tie each one closed with satin ribbon. Note: For a more frilly look, arrange lace netting around the sachets in the basket.

While expensive, perfectly coordinated tree ornaments almost always look stunning on a holiday tree, you can create the same effect with inexpensive ornaments decorated with potpourri.

MATERIALS: Potpourri of your choice*, glass ornaments, narrow satin ribbon, dried celosia, blue salvia, lavender, larkspur, globe amaranth, pepper grass, feverfew, and baby's breath, craft glue

*The potpourri shown here was made from celosia, blue salvia, lavender, larkspur, globe amaranth, pepper grass, feverfew, and baby's breath.

STEPS: **1** Press the potpourri through the hole in the top of the ornament. **2** Glue a small loop bow and ribbon loop to the top of the ornament, and then glue dried flowers under and around the bow.

These mischievous potpourri mice make fun surprises as stocking stuffers or tucked into children's closets.

MATERIALS: Potpourri of your choice, felt, cotton fabric, three small beads for each mouse, heavy thread, cotton balls

STEPS: **1** Cut two small circles about the size of a quarter and a long narrow tail from the felt. Photocopy the pattern pieces of page 141 and use them as a pattern to cut the cotton fabric. **2** Machine or hand sew the top two pieces together and press. Machine or hand sew the top and bottom together about three-fourths of the way around. Stuff the mouse with potpourri and cotton and then hand sew the top and bottom shut. **3** Sew or hot-glue the ears, eyes, and tail in place. To form the whiskers, thread a needle with heavy thread and run it through the fabric above the nose. Cut the thread at the desired length and repeat two more times.

Holiday knickknacks can be made from everyday items and materials found around your home in just a few minutes, and add the spirit of the holiday plus a wonderful fragrance wherever they're displayed.

MATERIALS AND STEPS FOR THE WREATH (top left): Fill two muslin squares with potpourri and tie them closed with satin ribbon. Hot-glue the sachets to a small vine wreath base, and then decorate the bottom of the wreath with small stems of dried German statice and satin ribbon.

MATERIALS AND STEPS FOR THE BEAR (top right): Dab a small amount of craft glue on the paws and feet of a small stuffed bear. Press potpourri into the glue and allow to dry completely. Tie a long satin ribbon in a bow around the bear's neck. Loop the ribbon ends down to the bear's feet and hot-glue in place.

MATERIALS AND STEPS FOR THE GHOST (lower left): Photocopy the pattern on page 141 and use it as a pattern to cut one layer of cotton. Place a small amount of potpourri in the top center of the fabric and tie closed with satin ribbon. Create the arms by gathering each side of the fabric and tying with ribbon. Add eyes with an ink marker.

MATERIALS AND STEPS FOR THE TREE (lower right): For the top horn, make a small sachet from the potpourri of your choice and a piece of netting and hot-glue it into the horn. For the lower horn, cut a piece of foam to fit inside the horn with a serrated knife and glue it into the horn. Cover the protruding foam with a thick layer of craft glue and press potpourri into the glue. Allow to dry completely and cover any bare spots with additional potpourri.

Simple holiday knickknacks are a fun way to decorate with small amounts of potpourri.

MATERIALS: Potpourri of your choice*, gold wishing well, small block of foam, craft glue

*The potpourri shown here contains rose petals, allspice berries, annual statice, and strawflowers.

STEPS: **1** Cut a piece of foam with a serrated knife to fit the inside of the wishing well. **2** Cover the top of the foam with a layer of craft glue and press the potpourri into the glue. Separate several small blooms from the potpourri, arrange them as desired, and glue in place. **3** Create a bow shape with petals from the potpourri and glue to the handle of the wishing well.

Afternoon Delights

The custom fit of this fragrant coat hanger was achieved with a glue gun instead of a special pattern or fancy sewing techniques.

MATERIALS FOR THE COAT HANGER: Potpourri of your choice, paper-covered coat hanger (from the dry cleaner's), adhesive spray, fabric, lace, braid, satin ribbon, glue gun

STEPS: **1** Spray the paper on both sides of the hanger with adhesive and roll the paper in potpourri. **2** Place the coat hanger in the center of your fabric. Fold the fabric over and around until it fits snugly. Trim any excess fabric away, fold the raw edges down, and secure in place with hot glue. **3** Fold a 2-inch (5-cm.) wide length of fabric in half and spiral it up and down the hood and neck of the hanger. Secure as needed with hot glue. **4** Decorate the hanger with lace, braid, and satin ribbon bows, securing them in place with hot glue.

MATERIALS FOR THE POTPOURRI PILLOWS: Potpourri of your choice, small scraps of fabric, fiber pillow filling, lace, narrow satin ribbon

See page 17 for complete instructions on making potpourri pillows.

Although you probably associate sachets with fabric or lace, they can also be made from paper ribbon, and make welcome additions to everyday table centerpieces.

MATERIALS: Potpourri of your choice, paper ribbon, 6- x 8-inch (15- x 20-cm.) block of floral foam, Spanish moss, floral pins, floral picks, dried silver dollar eucalyptus, German statice, rat tail statice, caspia, German statice, and sarrecena lilies, cinnamon sticks, raffia, glue gun

STEPS: **1** Cover the tops and sides of the foam base with floral pins. Attach the dried materials to floral picks. **2** Begin inserting picked materials into the foam to create the arrangement. Hot-glue the cinnamon sticks into the arrangement at an angle. **3** Cut the paper ribbon into eight squares. Fill each square with potpourri to form a sachet and tie it closed with raffia. **4** Hot-glue the sachets into the arrangement at varying angles and hot-glue a raffia bow in the center.

Baskets make wonderful vessels to display potpourri, and they can also be decorated with ribbons and stems of flowers and herbs to create lovely gifts and centerpieces.

MATERIALS FOR THE RASPBERRY COUNTRY GARDEN BASKET (far right): Potpourri of your choice (a pur-chased wood shaving potpourri is shown here), large pink basket, sheet moss, dried lavender, roses, celosia, larkspur, baby's breath, pepper-grass, pearly everlasting, strawflowers, feverfew, and globe amaranth, wide satin ribbon, glue gun

STEPS: **1** Cover the rim of the basket with sheet moss using hot glue. Position the focal flowers—the roses and celosia—evenly around the basket and hot-glue them in place. Then fill in remaining space with the other dried flowers. **2** Spiral a length of ribbon around the handle and hot-glue in place. Attach bows to both sides of the handle and then create an arrangement in the center of each bow with pearly everlasting and baby's breath.

MATERIALS FOR THE LAVENDER SWAG BASKET (right): Potpourri of your choice (a purchased wood shaving potpourri is shown here), gray basket, blue velvet ribbon, 20 stems of dried laven-der, dried boxwood foliage, and dried larkspur, floral wire, glue gun

STEPS: **1** Hot-glue a bow to one side of the basket. Arrange the stems of lavender into a swag and secure with floral wire. Position the swag over the bow and hot-glue in place. **2** Hot-glue accents of boxwood and larkspur around the swag and into the bow's loops.

83

MATERIALS FOR WEDDING BOUQUET: Dried rosebuds, carnations, globe amaranth, hydrangea, coneflowers, statice, black-eyed Susans, meadowsweet, bedstraw, sterlingia, larkspur, lavender, wild mint, 12-inch (30-cm.) stiffened doily, floral wire, floral tape, hot glue, several colors of tulle, narrow ribbon

STEPS: **1** Cut tulle into 11 2-inch (5-cm.) squares, one 4-inch (10-cm.) square, and five 3-inch (7-cm.) squares. Fill the 4- and 3-inch squares with a lavender and mint potpourri and twist each one closed with a length of floral wire. Gather each 2-inch square in the center and secure with floral wire to create small tufts. **2** Follow steps 1-3 below on how to make a tussie mussie.

MATERIALS FOR LAVENDER TUSSIE MUSSIE: German statice, peppermint leaves and blooms, lamb's ear, globe amaranth, senna pods, stiffened doily, floral wire, floral tape, hot glue, tulle, narrow ribbon

STEPS: **1** Cut tulle into four 2-inch (5-cm.) squares and one 3-inch (7-cm.) square. Fill each one with a lavender potpourri and twist closed with a length of floral wire. **2** Follow steps 1-3 below on how to make a tussie mussie.

MATERIALS FOR GOLDEN TUSSIE MUSSIE: Bay leaves, red peppers, rosebuds, santolina, rose hips, carnations, yarrow, black-eyed Susans, Queen Anne's lace, stiffened doily, floral wire, floral tape, hot glue, tulle, narrow ribbon

STEPS: **1** Cut a 2-inch (5-cm.) square from the tulle. Fill it with a strawflower and santolina potpourri and twist it shut with a length of floral wire. **2** Follow steps 1-3 below on how to make a tussie mussie.

HOW TO MAKE A TUSSIE MUSSIE

1 Attach the dried flowers and herbs that have stems to a length of floral wire and wrap with floral tape.

2 Arrange the potpourri sachets and wired flowers in a bouquet. Secure the stems together by wrapping with floral tape and push them through the center hole in the pre-stiffened doily. (Doilies can be stiffened with a mixture of sugar and water or with fabric stiffener.) Hot-glue a length of narrow ribbon to the floral tape at the top of the stems. Spiral the ribbon down the stems to cover the floral tape, hot-gluing as needed.

3 Hot-glue the flowers and herbs that don't have stems into the bouquet, and hot-glue the bow to the base of the tussie mussie. Add designer flairs by tying love knots in the ribbon or hot-gluing faux pearls or dried flowers into the ribbon if desired.

While most traditional wreaths are made by decorating the surface of the wreath's base, this wreath decorates the center of the base with a colorful potpourri.

MATERIALS: Potpourri of your choice*, dried globe amaranth blooms, 16-inch (41-cm.) grapevine wreath base, tulle or netting, cardboard, bow, craft glue, glue gun

*The potpourri shown here contains globe amaranth, annual statice, strawflowers, and lavender oil.

STEPS: **1** Cut out a circle of cardboard slightly smaller than the wreath. Then cut out two circles of tulle about an inch (2-1/2 cm.) larger than the cardboard. **2** Place one of the tulle circles on top of the cardboard. Fold the edges over and secure with craft glue. Cover this surface with potpourri and then glue the remaining tulle circle on top of the potpourri. Now hot-glue the potpourri circle to the back of the wreath base. **3** Hot-glue a bow to the top of the wreath and decorate the surface area of the wreath as desired.

Grow Your Own Roses

The rose (Rosa) has been treasured for its beauty and sweet fragrance for more than 5,000 years. It was strewn on the floors at Greek and Roman banquets, stored as potpourri by the Egyptians, and adopted as emblems by the feuding English houses of York and Lancaster. More than 5,000 varieties now exist, and the numerous shapes, sizes, colors, and fragrances are staggering.

General growing requirements include good drainage, at least six hours of sun a day, good air circulation, spring pruning, summer mulch, and winter protection. Roses can be propagated from seed, cuttings, and bud grafts, but the most reliable method is starting out with purchased stock.

Dry whole rose buds by hanging in small bunches or placing in a desiccant such as silica gel or sand. Individual petals can also be dried on a screen rack.

Potpourri crafts are a natural choice for decorating the bathroom because the moist air helps release the fragrances.

MATERIALS FOR THE BATH BAGS (left): Potpourri of your choice*, several colors of lace, narrow satin ribbon, and tulle, glass jar, 1 cup (250 ml.) lavender

*The potpourri shown here was made with lavender, rosemary, thyme, basil, peppermint, lemon and orange rinds, rose scented geranium leaves.

STEPS: **1** Cut the lace and tulle into squares measuring 3 x 6 inches (7 x 15 cm.). Place the tulle over the lace, fold in half, and sew sides and bottom closed. **2** Fill the sachets with potpourri and tie the bags closed with satin ribbon. Arrange a layer of dried lavender blooms on the bottom of a decorative jar and place the completed bath bags on top of the lavender. **3** Add fragrance to your bath water by placing a single bag in the tub under running water. Each bag may be reused until the fragrance diminishes.

MATERIALS FOR THE DECORATED BASKET (right): Potpourri of your choice*, small box with lid, lace, narrow velvet ribbon, glue gun, and small stems of dried strawflowers, roses, larkspur, celosia, globe amaranth, and baby's breath

*This potpourri was purchased in the linen section of a department store.

STEPS: **1** Glue the lace around the sides and top of the basket. Position a length of velvet ribbon in the center of the lace and secure with hot glue. **2** Decorate the top of the basket by first creating a center arrangement of celosia, two strawflowers, and a single rose and hot-gluing in place. Next, fill out the sides of the arrangement by hot-gluing larkspur, globe amaranth, baby's breath, and roses around the center flowers.

A cup of potpourri, soap and fabric scraps, and some imagination are all you need to create fragrant accents for your bathroom.

MATERIALS FOR THE TISSUE BOX: Potpourri of your choice*, satin ribbon, braid, cardboard tissue box, spray adhesive, glue gun, acrylic spray

*The potpourri shown here contains rose petals, leaves, and buds.

STEPS: **1** Spread a layer of potpourri out on a newspaper. Working in a well-ventilated area, spray the sides and top of the box with spray adhesive. Press each side of the box into the potpourri. **2** Spray the potpourri with a protective layer of acrylic spray and allow to dry completely. Using hot glue, decorate each side of the box with braid and bows.

MATERIALS FOR THE SOAP BALLS: Potpourri of your choice*, whole bars or scraps of soap

STEPS: **1** Shave the soap into small slivers and place them in a microwave-safe bowl. Add a teaspoon (7 ml.) of water for each cup (250 ml.) of soap and microwave on a medium temperature setting for two minutes or until the soap begins to bubble up and rise like a souffle.

2 Remove the soap from the microwave and stir with a butter knife. The soap is ready when it reaches the consistency of cake frosting. Add additional water and microwave again if necessary. **3** Press the soap out flat on a sheet of wax paper and sprinkle with potpourri. Then use your hands to form small soap balls. The soap hardens fast so you will need to work quickly. The soaps can be decorated with whole blooms from the potpourri if desired.

90

A simple Valentine candy box becomes a special hideaway for jewelry and other keepsakes when decorated with potpourri, velvet, and trimmings.

MATERIALS FOR THE HEART BOX: Potpourri of your choice*, heart-shaped candy box (other kinds and shapes of boxes work just as well), velvet, lace, narrow satin ribbon, pink spray paint, spray adhesive, glue gun

*The potpourri shown here contains rose petals, leaves, and whole blooms.

STEPS: **1** Arrange a lining of velvet on the insides of both box pieces and secure in place with hot glue. **2** Spray-paint the top of the box and allow to dry completely. Then coat it with a layer of spray adhesive and cover with potpourri. **3** Using hot glue, decorate the top of the box with ribbon, bows, and lace.

MATERIALS FOR THE HAT AND BASKET JEWELRY: Potpourri of your choice*, hat and basket miniatures, broach pin backing, narrow satin ribbon, pink spray paint, glue gun, craft glue

STEPS: **1** Spray-paint the miniatures and allow to dry completely. **2** Decorate the rim of the hat by applying a layer of craft glue and gently pushing the potpourri into it. Decorate the basket by gluing whole petals of potpourri inside the container. **3** Hot-glue the hat and basket together and attach small satin ribbons.

MATERIALS FOR THE LACE AND POTPOURRI BROACH: Potpourri of your choice*, broach pin backing, narrow lace, clear acrylic spray, craft glue, glue gun

STEPS: **1** Gather the lace and hot-glue it to the back side of the broach pin backing. **2** Cover the top surface area of the broach with a layer of craft glue and gently push the potpourri into it. Position a single rose bud in the center of the potpourri and glue it in place. **3** Allow the glue to dry completely and then spray with a protective layer of clear acrylic.

Although the most popular way of displaying potpourri is with the materials mixed together, they can also be separated and arranged in pretty layers in glass jars and bottles. These layered potpourris make entertaining projects for restless kids on rainy afternoons.

MATERIALS: Potpourri of your choice*, glass jar, lace, ribbon, or raffia to decorate the jar if desired

*Left: thyme, rose hips, roses, carnations, rose oil

*Far left: juniper berries, roses, red peppers, German statice, globe amaranth, sea oats, cinnamon sticks, carnations, cinnamon oil, pine oil, rose oil

*Below: roses, Queen Anne's lace, black-eyed Susans, star anise, day lilies, lavender, hydrangea, rose hips, fuchsia, oak moss, senna pods

STEPS:
1 Layer the potpourri in a jar one material at a time. Very light materials, such as finely crushed petals or leaves, should be placed at the bottom to prevent them from gradually shifting downwards. 2 Add several drops of essential oil and decorate the jar if desired.

This creative version of the traditional craft topiary is simpler to make than you might imagine, and the classic leather ladies' glove was an inexpensive find in an antique store.

MATERIALS: Potpourri of your choice*, clay pot, plaster of Paris, 14-inch (36-cm.) metal dowel, 4-inch (10-cm.) foam ball, 16-inch (41-cm.) glove, 4-inch wide lace, narrow satin ribbon, garden wire (used to train plants and available at garden centers), glue gun, craft glue

*The potpourri shown here contains hydrangea, zinnias, strawflowers, roses, German statice, globe amaranth, larkspur, and pearly everlasting.

STEPS: **1** Prepare the base of the topiary as directed below. **2** Trace the shape of the glove onto a sheet of paper. Beginning at the left side of the wrist, shape the wire up and around the fingers to match the tracing. When you've completed the fingers, twist the wire together at the wrist, and then continue twisting the wire down the dowel. **3** Add shape to the hand by hot-gluing cotton around the wire fingers. Fit the glove over the wire form. Use the point of a pencil to stuff additional pieces of cotton into the glove if needed. **4** Cover the base of the glove with lace and fold slightly over the top edge of the pot. Glue in place. Arrange another length of lace around the bottom of the pot. Glue in place and add ribbon bows as desired. **5** Glue the foam ball inside the palm of the glove and shape the fingers around the ball. Cover the ball with craft glue and press the potpourri gently in place. **6** Finish the topiary by trailing several potpourri blooms down the wrist and filling the base of the topiary with loose potpourri.

PREPARING A TOPIARY BASE:

*For a large topiary, position a dowel (or stem) in your container and pour plaster of Paris around it.

*For a small topiary, cut a piece of foam to fit inside your container and secure in place with hot glue. Insert the dowel (or stem) into the foam. Remove it, fill the hole with hot glue, and then reinsert it.

A large glass vase makes an ideal container for a layered potpourri made from dried spring and summer flowers, allowing you to enjoy the beauty of your favorite garden flowers through the winter.

MATERIALS: Potpourri of your choice*, large glass vase

*The potpourri shown here contains mountain mint, spearmint, chamomile, lavender, roses, lemon verbena, zinnias, oak leaves, larkspur, holly, peppergrass, and rat tail statice.

STEPS: **1** Sort the materials into piles and determine which order you will layer them in. The most fragrant materials should be near the top and materials should contrast in color, shape, and/or texture. **2** Layer the materials in the vase until it is full.

97

Crocheted doilies are a lovely alternative to fabric for encasing potpourri, and their lacy appearance invites whimsical ribbon and flower decorations.

MATERIALS FOR MAGENTA RIBBON DOILY: 1-1/2 cups (375 ml.) of the potpourri of your choice*, dried globe amaranth, wild mint, peppermint, meadowsweet, 11-inch (27-cm.) lace doily, 18-inches (46 -cm.)

HOW TO MAKE
A DOILY SACHET

1 Use your doily as a guide to cut a circle of tulle about a half-inch (1-1/4 cm.) smaller than the doily. **2** Place your pot-pourri on one side of the tulle. Fold the tulle in half and hot-glue the edges closed.
3 Place the potpourri bag on the wrong side of the doily, and fold the doily in half over the bag. Secure the outer edges of the doily shut with ribbon or hot-glue and decorate as desired.

of plastic beads, ivory tulle, narrow satin ribbon, medium-gauge floral wire, hot glue

*The potpourri in this doily was made from strawflower petals, rose petals, buds, and hips, globe amaranth, and rose oil.

STEPS: **1** Follow the general instructions below on how to make a doily sachet. **2** Weave the ribbon through every other hole on the outer edge of the doily and through two rows in the center of the doily. When you've finished weaving, tie a knot at the end of each piece of ribbon. Trim the ribbon to a length you find attractive and tie additional knots in the middle and on the ends of the ribbon if you like. **3** Cut a 4-inch (10-cm.) square of tulle and gather it in the center of the square. Hold the gathers in place by twisting a short length of floral wire around them and hot-glue the tulle to the top of the doily. **4** Hot-glue a small loop bow to the center of the tulle. Then curve the beads into several loops and hot-glue them under the tulle. Last, hot-glue the blooms and leaves into and around the bow.

MATERIALS FOR BLUE RIBBON DOILY SACHET: 1 cup (250 ml.) of the potpourri of your choice*, dried lavender, 7-inch (17-cm.) lace doily, white tulle, narrow satin ribbon

*The potpourri in this doily was made from lavender, roses, peppermint, and rose and lavender oils.

STEPS: **1** Follow the general instructions below on how to make a doily sachet. **2** Weave the ribbon through every other hole on the outer edge of the doily. When you've finished weaving, tie a knot at the end of each piece of ribbon. Trim the ribbon to a length you find attractive and tie additional knots in the middle and on the ends of the ribbon if you like. **3** Hot-glue a small loop ribbon to the doily. Next make a lavender sachet made from a 4-inch (10-cm.) square of tulle. Tie the sachet closed with a short piece of ribbon and hot-glue it into the center of the bow.

MATERIALS FOR RED RIBBON DOILY: 1-1/2 cups of the potpourri of your choice*, cinnamon sticks, star anise, 10-inch (25-cm.) lace doily, white and red tulle, two colors of narrow satin ribbon, medium-gauge floral wire, hot glue

*The potpourri in this doily was made from peppermint, anise leaves, yarrow, cinnamon chips, star anise, rose petals, fuchsia, lamb's ear, and rose, cinnamon, and anise oils.

STEPS: **1** Follow the general instructions below on how to make a doily sachet. **2** Weave the ribbon through every other hole on the outer edge of the doily and through a row near the center of the doily. When you've finished weaving, tie a knot at the end of each piece of ribbon. Trim the ribbon to a length you find attractive and tie additional knots in the middle and on the ends of the ribbon if you like. **3** Cut a 4-inch (10-cm.) square of red tulle and gather it in the center of the square. Hold the gathers in place by twisting a short length of floral wire around them and hot-glue the tulle to the top of the doily. **4** Hot-glue a small loop bow to the center of the tulle. Last, hot-glue cinnamon sticks and star anise to center of the bow, and hot-glue a few cinnamon chips to the bow's streamers.

Just a few simple embellishments—lace, ribbon, and dried flowers—transforms ordinary fabric sachets into memorable gifts and fragrant accents for the guest bedroom.

MATERIALS FOR THE TOP ROW OF SACHETS: Fabric sachet bag, lace, narrow satin ribbon, miniature rosebuds; (middle) fabric sachet bag, ribbon, silver king artemisia, larkspur, lavender; (right) fabric sachet bag, ribbon, silver king artemisia, lavender, cockscomb, rosebud

MATERIALS FOR THE BOTTOM ROW OF SACHETS: Fabric sachet bag, ribbon, cockscomb, baby's breath, rosebuds, larkspur; (middle) fabric sachet bag, lace, narrow satin ribbon, globe amaranth, peppermint leaves; (right) fabric sachet bag, ribbon, globe amaranth, baby's breath, larkspur

STEPS: **1** Follow the instructions on page 16 to make the sachet bags. **2** Decorate the bags with gathers of lace, ribbon streamers, and/or dried flowers.

101

While not edible, potpourri confections make lovely party decorations and hostess gifts for wedding and baby showers.

MATERIALS: Potpourri of your choice, whole bars or scraps of soap, candy or cupcake wrappers, craft glue

STEPS: **1** Shave the soap into small slivers and place in a microwave-safe bowl. Add a teaspoon (7 ml.) of water for each cup (250 ml.) of soap and microwave on a medium temperature setting for two minutes or until the soap begins to bubble up and rise like a souffle. **2** Remove the soap from the microwave and stir with a butter knife. The soap is ready when it reaches the consistency of cake frosting. Add additional water and microwave again if necessary. **3** Fill the cupcake and candy liners with the soap mixture. *Tip*: The soap hardens quickly so you will need to work fast. **4** Use craft glue to decorate the tops of the confections with whole blooms from your favorite potpourri. For the confections shown here, a bar of pink soap was shaved into powder and then sprinkled over the potpourri as an extra touch.

Note: Be sure to keep the confections out of the reach of young children—they may look real but they do taste awful!

A warm, spicy fragrance will fill the room when you entertain with a hot plate and coaster set filled with potpourri. Although these colors were chosen with Christmas in mind, you could easily select colors to complement a favorite set of dishes or table linens.

MATERIALS FOR THE HOT PAD: Christmas potpourri (see page 23 for recipe), cotton fabric in a holiday pattern, quilt batting, gold thread

STEPS: **1** Cut two layers of fabric and two layers of batting in the shape of a circle. Pin the batting to the wrong side of the fabric circle that will be the bottom of the hot pad. Stitch the layers together with the fabric facing right sides together. Leave an opening about 2 inches (5 cm.) long. **2** Turn the hot pad right sides out and fill with potpourri. (Note: The hot pad will release more fragrance if the potpourri is placed on top of the batting.) Fold the edges of the opening under and stitch closed by hand. **3** Create a quilted effect by running a single strand of gold thread down through the layers and back up again and then tying the two threads together in several knots.

MATERIALS FOR THE COASTER HOLDER: Christmas potpourri, plain coaster holder (can be cut from a box if necessary), small square of green cotton fabric or felt, red lace, gold thread

STEPS: **1** Cut a square of red lace and green fabric or felt to fit the bottom of the coaster holder. Sprinkle a layer of potpourri over the green square and cover it with the red lace square. Sew the two squares together with a top stitch. **2** Measure the distance of one side of square and then cut a length of lace six times longer. Gather the lace and stitch it to the sides of the square. Last, make four small bows from the gold thread and stitch one to each corner.

Hundreds of years ago, citrus pomander balls were worn as necklaces and belt decorations to ward off infections and the smell of raw sewage. Today, pomanders are a favorite holiday tradition, and they're easy to decorate with small sachets.

MATERIALS FOR ORANGE RIBBON POMANDER (bottom right): Orange, (or other citrus fruit), cloves, narrow satin ribbon, cotton print ribbon, lace, sewing pins, glue gun

STEPS: **1** Follow the directions on page 107 for how to make a pomander. **2** Position the print and satin ribbons around the pomander. Secure with sewing pins and hot glue. Make a small loop bow and hot-glue it to the top of the pomander. **3** Cut a 2-inch (5-cm.) square of lace and fill it with whole star anise. Tie the sachet shut with ribbon and tie it to the bow.

MATERIALS FOR LACE SACHET POMANDER (bottom left): Orange (or other citrus fruit), cloves, narrow satin ribbon, two kinds of lace ribbon, ivory tulle, sewing pins, glue gun

STEPS: **1** Follow the directions on page 107 for how to make a pomander. **2** Position the lace ribbon around the pomander. Secure with sewing pins and hot glue. Make a small loop bow and hot-glue it to the top of the pomander. **3** Cut a 2-inch (5-cm.) square of tulle and fill it with cloves. Tie the sachet shut with satin ribbon and tie it to the bow.

MATERIALS FOR RED AND GREEN POMANDER (top): Orange, cloves, plaid cotton ribbon, two colors of narow satin ribbon, pipe cleaner, red tulle, sewing pins, glue gun

STEPS: **1** Follow the directions on page 107 for how to make a pomander. **2** Position the plaid cotton ribbon around the pomander. Secure with sewing pins and hot glue. Cut the pipe cleaner into 3-inch (7-cm.) lengths and curve into loops. Hot-glue the loops to the top of the pomander and hot-glue a small loop bow in the center of the pipe cleaners. **3** Trim two lengths of narrow ribbon to 12 inches (30 cm.)

and secure them at their half-way point to the bottom of the orange with a sewing pin and hot glue. Cut four 1-inch (2-1/2-cm.) squares of tulle, fill them with potpourri, and tie to the bottom of each ribbon.

HOW TO MAKE A RIBBON POMANDER

1 Pin two lengths of ribbon around the orange to divide it in quarters. Punch holes in the orange 1/4-inch (3/4-cm.) apart in the areas not covered with ribbon. **2** Remove the ribbon from the orange and insert cloves in all the holes. Place the orange in a plastic bag with a mixture of two tablespoons (28 ml.) cinnamon powder, two tablespoons orris root powder, and two drops of cinnamon or clove oil. Shake well. **3** Tap the orange to remove excess powder, wrap in tissue paper, and store in a dark place for two to three weeks to fix the fragrance. **4** Decorate and display as desired.

This small basket was designed to hang from a ceiling fan and adds a delicate fragrance to the air with every turn of the blades.

MATERIALS: Potpourri of your choice*, satin ribbon, silk rose buds, small basket, craft glue

STEPS: **1** Coat the outside of the basket and the handle with a thin layer of craft glue and press the potpourri into the glue. Allow the glue to dry completely and then fill in any bare spots with additional potpourri. **2** Arrange the silk flowers inside the basket and secure with glue. Tie a piece of ribbon in a small bow and glue to the side of the basket. **3** Wrap a second piece of ribbon around the top of the handle and secure in place by tying several knots. Tie the basket to the fan's pull cord or to one of the blades.

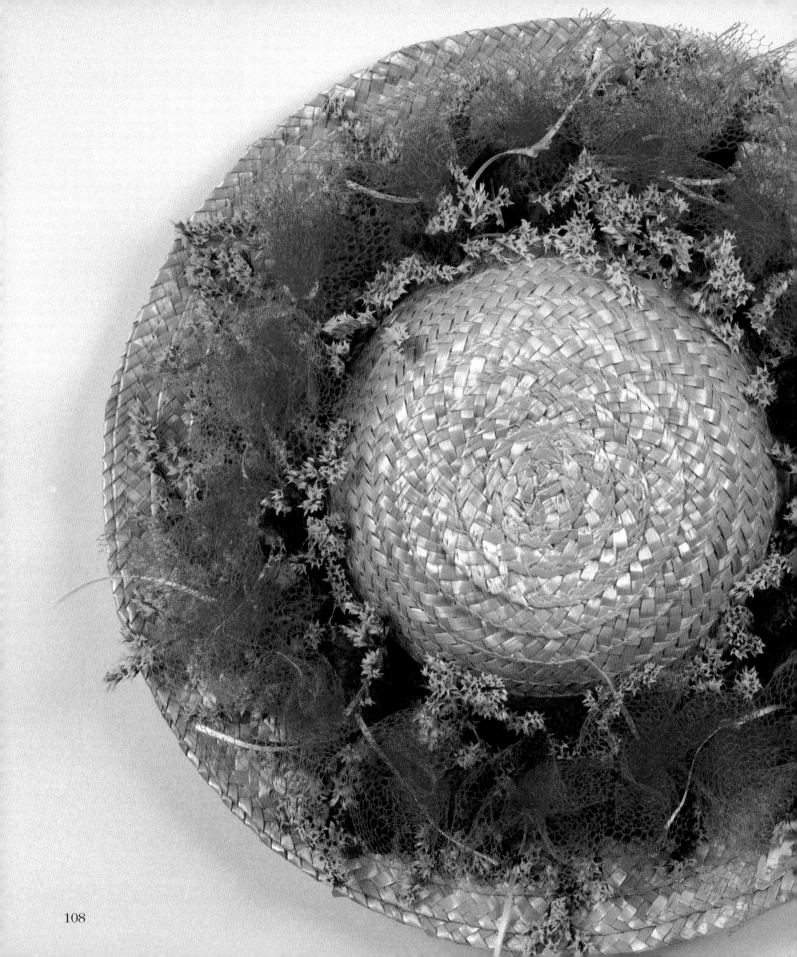

An inexpensive straw hat makes a creative base for a potpourri wall hanging and adds country charm to any room.

MATERIALS: Potpourri of your choice, straw, tulle, ribbon, hot glue, dried German statice and annual statice

STEPS: **1** Make enough sachets to go around the top of the hat by cutting the tulle into rectangular shapes, placing some potpourri in the center of each rectangle, and tying the sachets with ribbon. **2** Secure the sachets to the hat with a glue gun. **3** Position a row of German statice around both sides of the sachets and hot-glue in place. For extra color, hot-glue several stems of annual statice into the German statice.

Grow Your Own Lamb's Ear

This hardy perennial has thick, silver-colored wooly leaves and is also known by the common names of woundwort and rabbit ears. Once prized for its medicinal qualities, lamb's ear (Stachys lanata) was used as a poison antidote, as bandages, and even as protection against the evil eye.

A member of the mint family, the plant makes a nice mat edging in borders, and its tiny purple flowers frequently attract bees. Propagation is easiest from roots. Lamb's ear needs plenty of sun, moderately rich soil, and good drainage.

Dry the leaves by spreading them flat on a screen rack. Dry the blooms by hanging them in small bunches.

Grow Your Own Strawflowers

The annual strawflower (Helichrysum bracteatum) makes a cheerful addition to any rock garden or border. The daisy-like flowers bloom from mid to late summer and are among the most popular everlastings. They range in color from red to salmon to purple, to yellow, white, and pink.

A native of Australia, strawflowers can be propagated from seed or by division. The plants like well-drained, sandy soil and lots of sun.

Dry by hanging in small bunches or by arranging individual flower heads on a screen rack.

Inexpensive acrylic box frames provide an interesting surface area to decorate with potpourri. Although the photograph in this project was outlined with an oval shape, other, less traditional shapes, such as stars and flowers, would also be fun to try.

MATERIALS: Potpourri of your choice*, acrylic box frame, photograph, narrow lace, craft glue

*The potpourri in this project contained strawflowers, money plant, globe amaranth, wild basil blooms, miniature rose buds, anise hyssop blooms, annual statice, allspice berries, black-eyed Susans, and achillea 'The Pearl'.

STEPS: **1** Cut a piece of cardboard in an oval shape and position it in the center of the acrylic frame. Keep the cardboard in place and cover the remaining surface area with a layer of craft glue. Sprinkle a layer of dried sweet marjoram over the glue and press it gently in place. Remove the cardboard shape and allow to dry completely.
2 Outline the oval shape with dried purple statice (or another variety of dried flower) and then fill in the remaining area with assorted potpourri materials. Last, glue a row of lace around all four sides of the frame.

See page 112 for directions.

Strands of fabric with potpourri braided into them are as versatile as your imagination will allow: Hang them over bed posts, around door knobs, over the head rest in a car seat, or any other place you'd like to fragrance.

MATERIALS: Potpourri of your choice, fabric, narrow satin ribbon, adhesive spray, glue gun

STEPS: **1** Cut the fabric into three long strips about 2-1/2 inches (6 cm.) wide. Place them on a flat surface with the right sides facing down and coat with a fine layer of adhesive spray. **2** Sprinkle the potpourri down the middle of the strips. Fold the two raw edges in toward the center so that your strips now measure about an inch (2-1/2 cm.) wide. **3** Braid tightly until you reach the desired length. Secure in a circle with hot glue and decorate with a satin bow.

See page 111 for photograph of this project.

If you find that your potpourri-filled doilies are just too pretty to hide away in a drawer, you may want to display them on the wall.

MATERIALS: Potpourri of your choice, two cotton doilies, narrow satin ribbon, velour or velvet fabric, acrylic box frame, adhesive spray

STEPS: **1** Position the doilies on top of each other with a layer of potpourri in between and secure them together with narrow ribbon. (A large tapestry needle can be used if desired.) **2** Cut a piece of velour or velvet several inches than the size of the box and secure it inside with adhesive spray. Allow it to dry completely, and then glue the doily in the center of the box.

The recipient of this decorated Christmas package will enjoy the box at least as much as its contents, and the fragrant bow can be saved to wrap around a bed post or a vase.

MATERIALS: Potpourri of your choice*, enough velvet to cover the package, wide ribbon, narrow satin ribbon in two colors, two miniature baskets, glue gun, craft glue

*The potpourri shown here contains rose petals, leaves, and buds.

STEPS: **1** Wrap the package with the velvet fabric the same way you would if using ordinary gift paper. Secure with hot glue. Using the wide ribbon, decorate the top of the package with large ribbon loops and hot-glue them in place. **2** Holding two colors of narrow ribbon together, create seven small loops and hot-glue them into the loops of the wider ribbon. **3** Tie the two baskets to the handle with narrow ribbon. Fill each basket with rose petals and a single rose bud, and attach loose potpourri down the middle of the wide ribbon with craft glue.

Heart sachets don't always have to made from fabric. The heart sachets shown here were made from made from shelf lining paper and then attached to a length of lace to make a coordinating garland for a closet shelf.

MATERIALS: Potpourri of your choice, shelf lining or gift wrap paper, pre-gathered lace edging, narrow satin ribbon, hot glue

STEPS: **1** Photocopy the heart shape on page 141 and use it as a pattern to cut out six hearts. Place the hearts face down and put a small handful of potpourri in the center of three of the hearts. **2** Hot-glue the lace edging around the edges of the remaining three hearts and glue the hearts together. **3** Measure the length of your closet shelf and cut a length of lace to fit. Space the heart sachets evenly down the lace and hot-glue in place. Add small satin bows with hot glue and then secure the garland to your shelf with push-pins or hot glue. This garland also looks lovely over a kitchen window or around a Christmas tree.

Deciding how to decorate with these potpourri roses may be the most fun you've had in ages. They can grace the branches of Christmas trees or the tops of gift packages, or be tucked into book cases or linen drawers, just to name a few of the possibilities.

MATERIALS: Potpourri of your choice*, silk flowers, satin ribbon, craft glue

*The potpourri shown here contains rose petals, foliage, and buds.

STEPS: **1** Remove the stem from a silk flower and fold the bottom petals down. Apply a small amount of craft glue to the inner portion of the petals and press potpourri into the glue. Allow to dry completely. **2** Continue pulling rows of petals down and decorating as directed above until you reach the center of the flower. Glue a single rose bud (or other whole flower from your potpourri) in the center of the flower. **3** Secure two lengths of sating ribbon to the back of the flower with glue, creating loops or bows if desired.

A basket of kissing balls makes a beautiful, fragrant centerpiece for a luncheon or shower, and as they leave each guest can choose a ball to bring home as a hostess gift.

MATERIALS: Three containers of potpourri in contrasting colors*, one dozen foam balls, one dozen lengths of satin ribbon each trimmed to 15 inches (39 cm.), basket, small lace tablecloth or piece of fabric, spray adhesive, glue gun

*The potpourris shown here were purchased in a five and dime store.

STEPS: **1** Working with one ball at a time, spray a foam ball with adhesive spray and roll it in potpourri. Allow the adhesive to dry completely and then fill in any bare spots on the balls with additional pieces of potpourri. **2** Position the bottom of each ball at the center of a piece of ribbon and secure the ribbon in place with a dab of hot glue. Bring the ribbon up and around the ball and tie it in a bow. **3** Line the basket with lace and fill it with the kissing balls.

All-Day Affairs

Made from sachets filled with a moth-repellent potpourri and decorated with cedar balls, this wreath was designed to hang in a clothes closet. The wreath can also be made in Christmas colors and filled with a more spicy potpourri to celebrate the holiday season.

MATERIALS: Moth-repellent potpourri (see page 45 for recipe), 10-inch (25-cm.) embroidery hoop, cotton fabric, cedar wood balls, raffia bow, glue gun

STEPS: **1** Make enough sachet bags to go around the entire wreath. Press the bags and fill them with potpourri. Sew each bag shut with a gathering stitch about an inch (2.5 cm.) from the top. Gather the bags and hot-glue to the embroidery hoop. **2** Arrange and hot-glue cedar wood balls around the wreath. Position the bow and glue in place.

Tip: If you don't have enough moth-repellent potpourri to fill all of the sachet bags, try filling a few bags with fabric or newspaper scraps.

Grow Your Own Globe Amaranth

Globe amaranth (Gomphrena globosa) is the only species of Gomphrena in cultivation. Its botanical name "amaranthus" means unchangeable, and the clover-like flowers of this half-hardy annual make fine everlastings.

A summer bloomer, globe amaranth provides a lively splash of color to the late-season garden: purple, gold, magenta, white, and pink varieties are available. The plants love sun, tolerate drought well, and are easily propagated from seed.

Dry by hanging in small bunches or by arranging individual blooms on a screen rack.

Many people are amazed at how simple it is to add fragrant potpourri to holiday sewing projects. The traditional evergreen and spice potpourri in this stocking and ornament will be naturally fragrant the first year, and can be rejuvenated with a few drops of cinnamon oil in years to come.

MATERIALS FOR THE TREE ORNAMENT: Potpourri of your choice*, foam ball, cotton fabric, lace, gold cord, sequin-studded sewing pins, tulle or netting, hot glue

*The potpourri in this ornament was made from Christmas tree clippings, cinnamon chips, star anise, allspice berries, orange peel, and cloves.

STEPS: **1** Cut four 2-inch (5-cm.) squares of netting and top stitch them together on three sides to make two sachets. Fill each sachet with potpourri (do not overstuff) and sew closed on the fourth side. Pin one sachet to the center of each side of the ball. **2** Photocopy the pattern on this page and cut out fabric. Follow the folding instructions and position over the ball as directed. Secure each piece in place with sequin-studded pins. **3** Decorate the ball with lace and gold cord and secure in place with hot glue. (Note: Be especially careful to avoid glue burns since you're working with small pieces.)

MATERIALS FOR THE STOCKING: Potpourri of your choice, purchased or handmade stocking, length of fine-netting lace 4 inches (10 cm.) wide, gold cord, glue gun

STEPS: **1** Position the lace around the top of the stocking about 2 inches (5 cm.) deep and stitch or hot glue in place. Fill the space between the stocking and the lace with potpourri. **2** Fold the top of the lace over the top of the stocking and secure in place on the wrong side with hot glue. Decorate with gold cord, bows, and fabric decorations as desired.

FOLD IN HALF
VERTICALLY TO FIND
THE MIDDLE POINT
AND MARK
WITH A PIN.

RE-FOLD IN HALF
HORIZONTALLY
AND PRESS WITH
A HOT IRON.

A   B
FOLD CORNERS
A AND B TO THE
CENTER MARK
AND PRESS WITH
A HOT IRON.

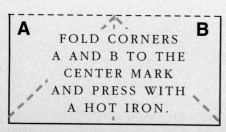

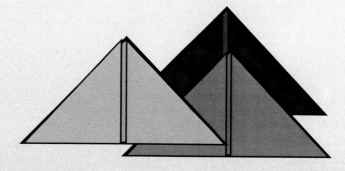

121

Filling sleep pillows with fragrant rose petals dates back to the early Romans, and through the centuries the pillows of kings and commoners alike have been filled with lady's bedstraw, scented grasses, lavender, hop, and numerous herbs. Today's sleep pillows tend to be much smaller than their historical counterparts, and are more likely to be designed for decorative, rather than functional, reasons.

MATERIALS: Potpourri of your choice*, linen and/or crocheted doilies, small scraps of lace from sewing projects or purchased in antique stores, natural fiber fabric (cotton, linen, silk) for portions of the top and the back of the pillows, cotton quilt batting

*The potpourri shown in the pillows on these and the following two pages contains roses, annual statice, globe amaranth, and strawflowers. Fragrant oils were not used to prevent the possibility of the laces being stained.

Follow the general instructions on page 17 for making the pillows.

Antique laces, as well as other sewing embellishments such as French hand sewing, cross stitch, and embroidery, are particularly well suited to the size and inherent charm of sleep pillows. Be careful to avoid potpourris scented with oils to prevent stains, and always allow your piece of fabric or lace to determine the finished size and shape of your pillow (or sachet) instead of cutting them down to fit the dimensions called for in a specific pattern.

The antique laces and fabrics on pages 122 and 123 include the doilies, left page, circa 1940; top right, French Valenciennes lace, circa 1900. The antique laces and fabrics on these pages include the lace and sewing scraps, left page, circa 1900; top right, Alencon galloon lace scraps from a 1905 wedding dress and antique silk piping.

The creative design of this rustic flower box allows you to combine the beauty of fresh flowers and colorful potpourri in one centerpiece.

MATERIALS: Potpourri of your choice*, moss, dried mushrooms, two tall glass vases, hot glue

*The potpourri shown here contains strawflowers, globe amaranth, and annual statice.

STEPS: **1** Line all four sides of the flower box with moss and secure as needed with hot glue. Next, create a more natural appearance by hot-gluing several dried mushrooms into the moss at varying angles. **2** Position a tall glass vase on each end of the flower box. Fill in the space between the vases with enough moss to keep the vases in an upright position. **3** Arrange fresh flowers in each vase and fill the center of the arrangement with a colorful potpourri.

Grow Your Own Globe Thistle

In spite of its genus name Echinops (Greek for hedge-hog-like), the steel blue summer flowers of the globe thistle are surprisingly soft to the touch. A hardy perennial, these tall plants make stunning back-row borders, and will attract a healthy bee population as well. Species vary in height.

Globe thistles can be propagated by division or grown from seed, and prefer light to medium soil and full sun. They do not thrive in severe cold or very wet areas.

Dry by hanging in small bunches or by arranging individual blooms on a screen rack.

Grow Your Own Peppermint

According to Greek mythology, Pluto (god of the underworld) fell in love with a nymph named Mintho, and Pluto's jealous wife wreaked revenge by changing poor Mintho into a lowly plant.

Peppermint (Mentha piperata) is a perennial herb, both flavorful and pungently aromatic. Its essential oils are used in medicines, chewing gums, candies, and alcoholic liqueurs, and the leaves make a refreshing tea.

Dry by hanging stems in small bunches or by spreading individual leaves flat on a screen rack.

The small muslin sachets in this culinary table wreath and kitchen garland were shaped to resemble cloves of fresh garlic.

MATERIALS FOR WREATH: Potpourri of your choice, grapevine wreath base, floral picks, seven 3 by 3-inch (7 x 7-cm.) squares of muslin, raffia, glue gun, fresh anise hyssop blooms, fennel, purple sage, garden sage, summer savory, oregano blooms, thyme, and basil, glue gun

STEPS: **1** Place a small amount of potpourri in the center of each square of muslin and tie closed with raffia. Mold the potpourri in the sachets until their shapes resemble small cloves of garlic. **2** Attach the fresh materials to floral picks and insert them into the wreath base, covering the outer and inner edges first and the top surface last. **3** Position the sachets at varying angles and hot-glue in place.

MATERIALS FOR SWAG: Potpourri of your choice, lamp wicking or cotton braid, chili hot peppers, five 3 x 3-inch (7 x 7-cm.) squares of muslin, raffia, glue gun

STEPS: **1** Place a small amount of potpourri in the center of each square of muslin and tie closed with raffia. Mold the potpourri in the sachets until their shapes resemble small cloves of garlic. **2** Hot-glue the sachets down the base and embellish with dried chili peppers.

A wicker bird cage decorated with potpourri will quickly become the envy of every bird in your neighborhood, not to mention provide for some interesting dinner conversations.

MATERIALS: Potpourri of your choice*, bird cage, floral foam, silk flowers and greenery, ribbon, craft glue, glue gun

STEPS: **1** Working with one section of the cage at a time, apply a thick layer of craft glue and press the potpourri into it. **2** Create a thatched roof effect by arranging honesty (or other potpourri material) and gluing in place. Select small blooms and petals from the potpourri and glue around the cage. **3** Cut a block of floral foam to fit inside the cage and insert silk flowers, greenery, and ribbon curls into it to create an arrangement. **4** Trim several stems of the silk flowers and greenery to 6 inches (15 cm.) and arrange them on top of the bird cage with a bow. Secure in place with hot glue.

Embroiderers and cross-stitchers who find themselves frustrated with the limited ways available to display their finished work will enjoy making these small sachets as gifts and accents around the home.

MATERIALS: Potpourri of your choice, thin cotton fabric, cross-stitched or embroidered fabric

To avoid the possibility of the potpourri's essential oils from staining your handiwork, it's a good idea to make a liner for the sachet from a thin cotton fabric, or to use a potpourri recipe that is naturally fragrant without the use of oils. See page 16 for basic sachet making instructions.

With a little help from a professional framer, the materials in your favorite display potpourri can be showcased in a matching wallhanging.

MATERIALS: Potpourri of your choice*, contrasting fabric, shadow box frame, craft glue

*The potpourri shown here contains globe thistle, miniature rose buds, pussy willows, tiger lilies, honesty, blue salvia, rat tail statice, daisies, star anise, love-in-a-mist, anise hyssop, pinecones, dogwood blooms and seed pods, and wild flowers.

Bring your design idea and some fabric to a frame shop. After the shadow box frame has been prepared, arrange the potpourri materials until you're happy with the effect and then glue them in place.

A bowl of crystallized edible flower blossoms makes a lovely table centerpiece and an even lovelier dessert.

MATERIALS: Violet blossoms, Johnny-jump-up blossoms, 1 egg white, 1 tablespoon (14 ml.) of water, 1 cup (250 ml.) sugar

STEPS: **1** Rinse the fresh-cut blossoms in water and allow to dry. Beat the egg white and water together. Dip the blossoms in the egg mixture, roll them in sugar, and arrange them on a sheet of wax paper. **2** Sprinkle additional sugar over the blossoms if needed and refrigerate.

Turn the blossoms over the next day and again sprinkle with sugar. Continue turning the blossoms and sprinkling with sugar until they are completely dry (approximately three to four days).

133

This large sachet wreath makes a perfect project for a rainy afternoon, and is simple enough for even young children to help.

MATERIALS: Potpourri of your choice, straw wreath base, cotton fabric, tulle, narrow ribbon, corsage pins, large bow, glue gun

STEPS: **1** Cut the cotton fabric into long, narrow strips. Wrap the strips around the base at an angle so that no straw shows. Secure as needed with corsage pins. **2** Attach the bow to the top of the wreath with a glue gun. **3** Make enough sachets to cover the wreath by cutting tulle into rectangular shapes, placing potpourri in the center of each rectangle, and tying with ribbon. Secure each sachet to the wreath base with a corsage pin.

Grow Your Own Love-In-A-Mist

Love-in-a-mist (Nigella damascenea) is known by several other common names, including Jack-in-prison, devil-in-a-bush, and lady-in-the-bower. Nigella's blue or white flowers huddle in nests of thread-like leaves, and the plants produce dark seeds that smell and taste much like strawberries. (Ancient Egyptians sprinkled nigella seeds on bread, and the English believed that inhaling their fragrance would cure the common cold.)

Nigella will grow in poor, moderately dry soil, but dislikes acid soils and shade. The flowering period is brief, so seeds should be sown successively.

Dry by hanging in small bunches.

Grow Your Own Marigolds

The Spaniards first discovered marigolds in Mexico and smuggled the seeds back home. The common name marigold was derived from the Spanish practice of placing the blooms on the Virgin Mary's altars where they were called "Mary's Gold." In India, the blossoms are still woven into garlands as tokens of friendship, and their petals are often used to make dyes for coloring butter and cheeses.

Marigolds (Tagete) propagate easily from seed, and can grow in almost any soil as long as they have plenty of sun. The flowers range from yellow to pure red.

Dry by hanging in small bunches or by arranging individual blooms on a screen rack.

Rag dolls have been enchanting their makers since the days of the depression, and potpourri accessories such as purses, baskets, hats, sachets, and parasols make lovely complements.

MATERIALS FOR THE PARASOL (far left): Potpourri of your choice, small piece of lace fabric, pre-gathered lace edging, narrow satin ribbon, florist's wire, glue gun

STEPS: **1** Cut the lace fabric into a square measuring 8 inches x 8 inches (20 cm. x 20 cm.). Fold it in half and glue the sides together. **2** Curve the florist's wire into a hook shape to form the parasol's handle. Spiral the narrow satin ribbon down the wire and secure as needed with hot glue. **3** Position the bottom of the parasol's handle in the bottom of the lace and glue that edge closed. Fill this lace sachet about three-fourths full with potpourri and tie the sachet closed with satin ribbon.

MATERIALS FOR THE BASKET (left): Potpourri of your choice, small basket, small block of foam, craft glue

STEPS: **1** Cut the foam to fit the inside of the basket with a serrated knife. Coat the foam that protrudes from the basket with a thick layer of craft glue. **2** Press the potpourri into the glue and allow to dry completely. Fill any bare spots with additional potpourri. Tie the basket to the doll's arm with a length of satin ribbon or slip the handle over the doll's arm.

MATERIALS FOR THE HAT (page 138, left): Potpourri of your choice, small straw hat, craft glue

STEPS: **1** Cover the top of the hat with a circle of craft glue. Select several whole blooms from the potpourri and press them into the glue. **2** Fill any remaining bare spots with additional pieces of potpourri.

MATERIALS FOR THE PURSE (page 138, center): Potpourri of your choice, small piece of lace fabric, narrow satin ribbon, silk roses, glue gun

STEPS: **1** Photocopy the rectangle shape on page 141 and use it as a pattern to cut out the lace. **2** Fold the bottom of the lace upwards, leaving 2 inches (5 cm.) at the top. Hot-glue the lace in place, fill with potpourri, and hot-glue the sides together.

MATERIALS FOR THE BASKET (page 139, right): Potpourri of your choice, small basket, small block of foam, craft glue

STEPS: **1** Cut the foam to fit the inside of the basket with a serrated knife. Coat the foam that protrudes from the basket with a thick layer of craft glue. **2** Press the potpourri into the glue and allow to dry completely. Fill any bare spots with additional potpourri. Tie the basket to the doll's arm with a length of satin ribbon or slip the handle over the doll's arm.

SACHET

SLEEP PILLOW

LEAVE
TU

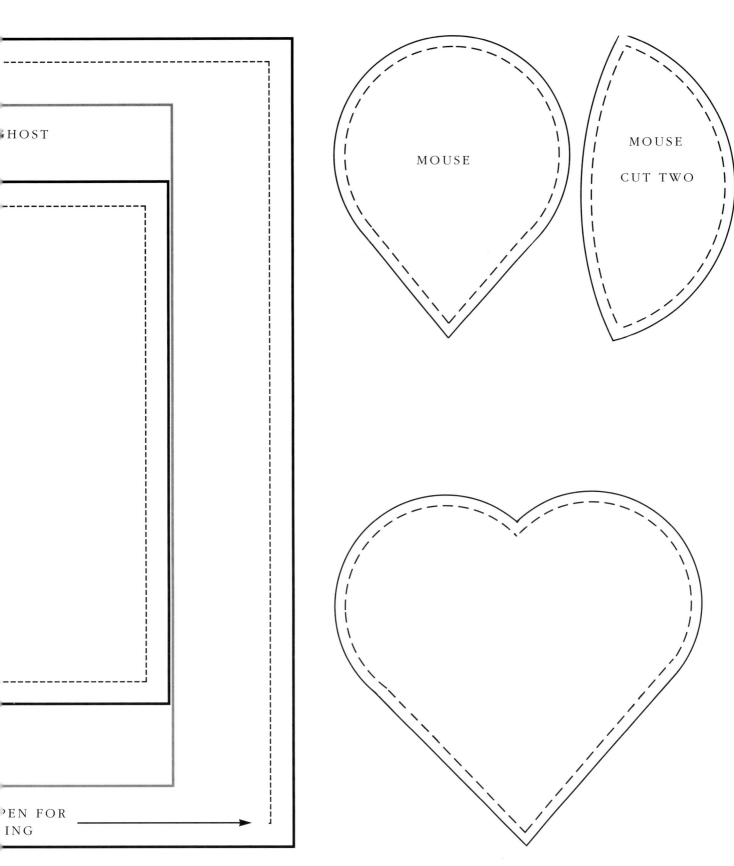

GHOST

OPEN FOR
ING

MOUSE

MOUSE
CUT TWO

Contributing Designers

NORA BLOSE (pages 23, 40, 42, 43, 44, 45, 62, 63, 64, 70, 71, 72, 73, 75, 76-top left and bottom left, 116, 128, 129, 133, 136, 138, and 139) gardens from her mountain home in western North Carolina, where she is well known for both her utilitarian and fragrant potpourris. She markets her potpourris and potpourri crafts under the name of "Nora's Follies."

DARLENE CONTI (pages 20, 60, 61, 68, 84, 85, 88, 94, 95, 98, 99, 100-top left and bottom middle, and 106) began making potpourris and potpourri crafts as a way to preserve the fragrance of her favorite flowers and herbs. She lives and gardens in Asheville, North Carolina.

JOYCE CUSICK (pages 122, 123, 124, and 125) grows a wide variety of roses in her gardens in Dunnellon, Florida. She is the owner of Historic Preservation, Inc., and specializes in historical surveying and planning.

JEANNETTE HAFNER (pages 74, 82, 83, 88, 89, 100-top right and lower left, and 101-top left and lower right) grows the plants for her potpourri in her garden in Orange Connecticut. She teaches flower and herb drying techniques as well as design classes, and sells her wreaths and potpourri crafts at craft fairs.

STEFFANY LABREE (pages 56, 76-lower right, 77, 110, 111, and 132) credits her inspirations to the activities of an overzealous dog, and her experiences of working in a frame shop. She is a full-time student majoring in Special Education.

DOT MCMULLEN (pages 104, 105, and 121) manages a fabric store and enjoys designing fun ways to mix sewing projects with naturally fragrant potpourris.

NICOLE VICTORIA (pages 65, 68, 69, 76-top right, 78, 79, 90, 91, 92, 93, 102, 103, 107, 112, 113, 114, 116, 117, and 115) specializes in Victorian crafts and markets a national wholesale line called "Nicole Victoria - Paris * 1893." Her favorite potpourri recipes are always made with bases of lavender and roses.

ALSO THANKS TO: Elizabeth Albrecht (pages 54, 56, 58, 59, 108, 119, 131, and 135); Margaret Albrecht (56, 108, and 135); Will Albrecht (page 56); Florence Brasier (pages 66 and 67); Constance Daly (page 135); Cynthia Gillooly of The Golden Cricket in Asheville, North Carolina (pages 80, 81, 127, and 131); Brenda LaBree (page 87); Seana LaBree (page 132); Sharon Lovejoy (page 51); Dot Rosenstengel (page 131); Diane Weaver of Gourmet Gardens in Weaverville, North Carolina (pages 36, 37, 96 and 97); Diane and Emmett Higgins; Quinlan House Antiques in Waynesville, North Carolina; and Stoll 'N Goods in Saegertown, Pennsylvania.

142

Botanical/Common Names

A
Allspice, *Pimenta dioica*
Anise hyssop, *Agastache foeniculum*
Annual statice, *Limonium sinuatum*

B
Bachelor's button, *Centaurea Cyanus*
Basil, Ocimum, *Clunopodium vulgare*
Bay leaves, *Laurus nobilis*
Bedstraw, *Galium*
Bee balm, *Monarda*
Bells-of-Ireland, *Molucella laevis*
Black-eyed Susans, *Rudbeckia hirta*
Blue salvia, *Salvia azurea*
Buttercups, *Ranunculus*

C
Calendula, *Calendula officinalis*
Carnations, *Dianthus spp.*
Cedar, *Cedrus*
Celosia, *Celosia cristata*
Chamomile, *Chamaemelum nobile*
Chenille plant, *Acalypha hispida*
Cherry, *Prunus ilicifolia*
Cinnamon, *Cinnamomum zeylanicum*
Cinnamon basil, *Ocimum basilicum var.*
Clove, *Syzygium aromaticum*
Cockscomb, *Celosia cristata*
Comfrey, *Symphytum officinale*
Coneflowers, *Echinacea angustifolia*

D
Daffodil, Narcissus, *pseudonarcissus*
Daisies, *Chrysanthemum Leucanthemum*
Daylily, *Hemerocallis minor*
Dogwood, *Cornus*
Dusty miller, *Artemisia stellerana*

E
Eucalyptus, *Eucalyptus*

F
Fennel, *Foeniculum vulgare*
Feverfew, *Chrysanthemum parthenium*
Fire thorn berries, *Pyracantha*
Foxglove, *Digitalis*
Fuchsia, *Fuchsia*

G
German statice, *Limonium tatarica*
Globe amaranth, *Gomphrena globosa*
Globe thistle, *Echinops ritro*

H
Hibiscus, *Hibiscus*
Holly, *Ilex*
Honesty, *Lunaria*
Honeysuckle, *Aquilegia canadensis*

I
Ivy, *Hedera*

J
Jasmine, *Jasminum*
Johnny-jump-up, *Viola pedunculata*
Juniper, *Juniperus*

L
Lamb's ear, *Stachys byzantina*
Larkspur, *Delphinium*
Lavender, *Lavandula*
Lemon balm, *Melissa officinalis*
Lemon basil, *Ocimum Americanum*
Lemon verbena, *Aloysia triphylla*
Locust, *Robinia*

Locust, honey, *Gleditsia, triacanthos*
Love-in-a-mist, *Nigella damascena*

M
Maple, *Acer*
Marigolds, *Tagetes*
Marjoram, sweet, *O. Majorana*
Mint, *Mentha*
Mountain laurel, *Kalmia latifolia*
Mountain mint, *Pycnanthemum spp.*

O
Oak leaf hydrangea, *Hydrangea*
Oregano, *Origanum spp.*
Orris, *Iris Xgermanica var. florentina*

P
Pansies, *Viola*
Parsley, *Petroselinum crispum*
Patchoili, *Pogostemum cablin*
Pearly everlasting, *Anaphalis*
Pennyroyal, *Mentha pulegium*
Peppergrass, *Lepidium*
Peppermint, *Mentha xpiperita*
Pincushion flower, *Leucospermum, Scabiosa*
Pussy willows, *Salix caprea*

Q
Queen Anne's lace, *Daucus carota*

R
Rose, *Rosa*
Rosemary, *Rosmarinus officinalis*

S
Saffron, *Carthamus tinctorius*
Sage, *Salvia*
Sandalwood, *Santalum*
Santolina, *Santolina chamaecyparissus*
Sarrecena lily, *Saraceniaceae*
Senna pods, *Cassia*
Scented geranium, *Pelargonium graveolens*
Scotch fir, *Pinus sylvestris*
Silver dollar eucalyptus, *Eucalyptus cinerea*
Silver king artemisia, *Artemisia ludoviciana*
Southernwood, *Artemisia Abrotanum*
Spanish moss, *Tillandsia usneoides*
Spearmint, *Mentha spicata*
Spice basil, *Ocimum spp.*
Star anise, *Foeniculum vulgare*
Statice, *Limonium*
Strawflowers, *Helichrysum bracteatum*
Summer savory, *Satureja hortensis*
Sweet Annie, *Artemisia annua*
Sweet marjoram, *Origanum Majorana*

T
Tansy, *Tanacetum vulgare*
Tarragon, *Artemisia dracunculus*
Thyme, *Thymus*
Tiger lily, *Lilium Catesbaei*
Tulip, *Tulipa suaveolens*

V
Vetiver, *Vetiveria zizanniodes*
Violet, *Viola*

W
Wormwood, *Artemisia, Vanilla barbellata*

Y
Yarrow, *Achillea*

Z
Zinnia, *Zinnia*

Mail Order Sources

Capriland's Herb Farm
Silver St.
North Coventry, CT 06238

Heart's Ease
4101 Burton Drive
Cambria, CA 93428-3003

Peqvea Trading Co.
10 East Main Street
Strasburg, PA 17579

Rasland Farm
N.C. 82 at U.S. 13
Godwin, NC 28344

Sandy Mush Herb Nursery
Route 2 Surrett Cove Road
Leicester, NC 28748

The Sassafrass Hutch
11880 Sandy Bottom, NE
Greenville, MI 48838

Sinking Springs Herb Farm
234 Blair Shore Rd.
Elkton, MD 21921

Smile Herb Shop
4908 Berwyn Rd.
College Park, MD 20740

Stillridge Herb Farm
10370 Rt. 99
Woodstock, MD 21163

Tom Thumb Workshops
P.O. Box 322
Chincoteague, VA 23336

Well-Sweep Herb Farm
317 Mt. Bethel Rd.
Port Murray, NJ 07865

Bibliography

Bailey, L.H. *Hortus Third*. New York: Macmillan Publishing Co., 1976.

Biles, Roy E. *The Complete Book of Garden Magic*. Chicago, Illinois: J.G. Ferguson Publishing Company, 1961.

Brownlow, Margaret. *Herbs and the Fragrant Garden*. London: Dartman, Longman, and Todd, 1963.

Bush-Brown, James & Louise. *America's Garden Book*. Revised edition by the New York Botanical Garden. Bronx, New York: Charles Scribner's Sons, 1980.

Coats, Alice M. *Flowers and Their Histories*. New York City, New York: Pitman Publishing Corporation, 1956.

Coats, Peter. *Flowers in History*. New York City, New York: Viking Press, 1970.

Duff, Gail. *A Book of Pot-Pourri*. New York City, New York: Beaufort Books Publishers, 1985.

Fields, Xenia. *Xenia Fields' Book of Garden Flowers: Perennials, Annuals and Biennials, and Other Attractive Garden Flowers*. London, England: Hamlyn, 1971.

Foster, Maureen. *The Flower Arranger's Encyclopedia of Preserving and Drying*. London: Blandford Press, 1988.

Heriteau, Jacqueline. *Potpourris and Other Fragrant Delights*. New York City, New York: Simon and Schuster, 1973.

Pickson, Margaret. *The Language of Flowers*. London, Great Britain: Michael Joseph Ltd.

Index